Generis
PUBLISHING

National Culture and the Private Saving Behavior

A Cross-Country Empirical Study

Anthony H. Tu
Nianzhi Guo

Title: **National Culture and the Private Saving Behavior**

A Cross-Country Empirical Study

ISBN: 979-8-89966-498-4

Author: Anthony H. Tu, Nianzhi Guo

Cover image: www.pixabay.com

Publisher: Generis Publishing
Online orders: www.generis-publishing.com
Contact email: info@generis-publishing.com

TABLE OF CONTENTS

ABSTRACT

This study investigates whether the culture of each country can explain the private savings behavior in that country. Attempts in prior studies to determine whether disparities in national saving rates can be explained by cultural attributes have been largely unsuccessful, mainly due to formidable problems related to the measurement of culture, data availability, and endogeneity. We extend prior research by employing the six measurable cultural dimensions of Hofstede et al. (2010), together with the largest currently available panel database covering 84 countries over the period 1981–2012. Using culture-related variables and saving rates, we test the hypothesis that cultural factors influence private saving behavior in an international context. We find that East Asian countries have the highest average private saving rates, followed by other Asian countries. Africa has the lowest private saving rate, while South America ranks second lowest. We then focus on four principal cultural variables—Confucianism, Long-Term Orientation (LTO), Uncertainty Avoidance (UA), and Indulgence versus Restraint (IVR)—and find that all four exert significant impacts on private saving rates worldwide. Our findings also help resolve the puzzle of why China, Japan, and other East Asian countries save so much and so persistently. Specifically, we find that high LTO scores in these regions are associated with high levels of private saving, while low UA scores help explain the persistence of high saving rates, even during periods of financial crisis. In addition, a restrained culture (low IVR) helps explain why other Asian countries exhibit the second-highest average private saving rates. In contrast, an indulgent culture (high IVR) combined with a short-term orientation (low LTO) helps explain why Africa and South America have lower average private saving rates.

Keywords: Long-term orientation; Uncertainty avoidance; Indulgence versus Restraint; Private saving; Confucianism.

1. INTRODUCTION[1]

Given the rapid growth of East Asian economies over recent decades, economists have paid increasing attention to the persistently high saving rates observed in these economies. In particular, the exceptionally high saving rates in China, Japan, and other East Asian countries have become an issue of considerable interest to policymakers and researchers around the world.

Although there has been considerable debate over why China saves so much—an issue commonly referred to as the "Chinese saving puzzle" (Modigliani and Cao, 2004)—this question has yet to be satisfactorily resolved in the literature.[2] In particular, important issues remain regarding why the focus has often been placed on the period up to 2008, just prior to the outbreak of the global financial crisis, during which China's saving rate peaked at 52%.[3] A number of studies have shown that the economies of China, Japan, and other East Asian countries have not only exhibited very high saving rates, but that these rates have also remained relatively stable over time.[4] In contrast, aggregate saving rates in Latin American countries tend to be low and relatively volatile.[5]

Although many potential explanations for cross-country differences in saving rates have emerged in the literature, the findings remain inconclusive (Wei and Zhang, 2011; Grigoli et al., 2018). The widely accepted determinants of saving behavior are generally associated with several factors, including inertia effects (Horioka and Wan, 2007), demographic factors (Wei and Zhang, 2011), fiscal policy (Lopez, Schmidt-Hebbel, and Serven, 2000), social security and pension systems (Cigno and Rosati, 1997; Bailliu and Reisen, 1998), foreign exchange reserves (Blanchard and Giavazzi, 2006), uncertainty (Leland, 1968; Bande and Riveiro, 2013; Levenko, 2020), national income levels and income growth (Bonham and Wiemer, 2013), and income inequality.[6]

---

[1] Portions of this article were previously published in Guo and Tu (2023).

[2] See, for example, Kraay (2000), Meng (2003), Modigliani and Cao (2004), Chamon and Prasad (2010) and Chao, Laffargue and Yu (2011).

[3] During the 2008 global financial crisis, the elevated savings rate can be partially attributed to an increased demand for precautionary savings (Mody, Ohnsorge and Sandri, 2012).

[4] Examples include Hayashi (1986), Horioka (1990), Edwards (1996), Dayal-Gulati and Thimann (1997), Adams and Prazmowski (2003) Chen, Imrohoroglu and Imrohoroglu (2006), He and Cao (2007), Horioka and Terada-Hagiwara (2012) and Grigoli, Herman and Schmidt-Hebbel (2018). As shown in Figure 1, nine countries in East Asia have not only enjoyed very high saving rates, but also stable trends in their saving rates. Exceptions to this are Japan and Hong Kong, both of which exhibited slight declines during our 1981-2012 sample period.

[5] See Edwards (1996), Dayal-Gulati and Thimann (1997) and Gutierrez (2007).

[6] Examples include Schmidt-Hebbel and Serven (2000), Li and Zou (2004), Chu and Wen (2017) and Gu, Tam, Li and Zhao (2020). A review of fifteen empirical studies of private saving rates is provided in Table 1 of Grigoli et al. (2018), which reveals considerable differences across these studies according to the various factors, including their sample size and coverage, data sources, saving rate definitions, model specifications and estimation methodologies.

Some earlier studies, such as Bosworth (1993), suggested that disparities in saving rates across countries may reflect cultural phenomena; that is, individuals in different countries may have distinct intrinsic motives or culturally specific reasons for saving. However, given the general view that national culture is an unobservable variable, the hypothesis that saving rates vary for cultural reasons is difficult to test using cross-country aggregate data.

Carroll, Rhee, and Rhee (1994) subsequently attempted to examine whether cultural factors influence saving behavior by comparing saving patterns in Canada among immigrants from countries with different saving rates. Their argument was that if a high saving rate is primarily a cultural phenomenon within a given country, then emigrants from that country who move to Canada should retain aspects of that culture. Accordingly, immigrants from high-saving countries would be expected to exhibit higher saving rates than immigrants from countries with lower saving rates. Using household data from the Canadian Survey of Family Expenditure (SFE), they tested for cultural effects on saving behavior. However, they found no significant differences in saving patterns among immigrant groups by country of origin, largely due to limitations in sample size and data availability.

Carroll, Rhee, and Rhee (1999) extended their earlier study by examining the same questions using household data from the 1980 and 1990 U.S. Censuses of Population and Housing (CPHUS). Unlike the SFE, the CPHUS census data included substantially larger immigrant samples and explicitly identified both country of birth and year of immigration. The results of this second study revealed significant differences in saving patterns among immigrants across countries of origin.

However, the saving patterns observed among immigrants in Carroll et al. (1999) did not correspond to the saving patterns in their countries of origin. In particular, immigrants from East Asian countries such as Japan, South Korea, and Taiwan did not exhibit higher saving rates than other immigrant groups in the sample. Overall, due to limited data availability and the inherent difficulties associated with measuring culture, their studies provided little empirical support for the hypothesis that cultural factors are important in explaining cross-country differences in saving rates.

More recently, Ye, Pan, Lian, and Ng (2020) investigated the relationship between culture and national saving rates using several (though not all) observable Hofstede cultural indices and macroeconomic data for 48 countries over the period 1990–2013. Employing Relative Importance Analysis, they found that culture-related variables—Uncertainty Avoidance, Individualism, and Long-Term Orientation—can explain the high saving rates observed in Asian countries and are among the most important determinants of saving, alongside economic growth, social security, and demographic factors. However, their study focused on national (rather than private) saving rates, and it did not address the determinants underlying the persistence of high saving rates.

Motivated by these prior studies, the present study pursues two specific objectives. The first is to extend earlier research by employing the largest dataset currently available, covering 84 countries over the period 1981–2012, to re-examine the effects of culture on disparities in private saving rates across countries. To address the issue of the non-observability of culture—which has constrained previous studies—we employ all six measurable cultural dimensions proposed by Hofstede (2001). These dimensions provide continuous score variables for a large number of countries and remain among the most widely cited measures in the cultural literature. Our results indicate that Uncertainty Avoidance, Long-Term Orientation, and Indulgence (but not Individualism) significantly explain cross-country disparities in private saving rates.

The six cultural dimensions proposed by Hofstede et al. (2010) are: Uncertainty Avoidance (UA), Individualism (IND) versus Collectivism, Power Distance (PD), Masculinity (MAS) versus Femininity, Long-Term Orientation (LTO) versus Short-Term Orientation, and Indulgence versus Restraint (IVR). All of these measures were originally constructed based on surveys conducted among IBM employees. The first four dimensions—UA, IND, PD, and MAS—constitute the original framework of Hofstede's "cultural consequences" (Hofstede, 1980, 1991, 2001), while LTO and IVR were added later.

Our second objective is to focus on four principal cultural variables in East Asian countries to explain why private saving rates are both exceptionally high and highly persistent in this region. The cultural core of China, Japan, and other East Asian countries can be characterized by Confucianism, high LTO, and low UA and IVR.[7] Confucianism represents a common cultural foundation across China, Japan, and many other East Asian societies. Countries and regions strongly influenced by Confucian traditions include China, Taiwan, Hong Kong, Macau, South Korea, Japan, and Vietnam, as well as territories with significant ethnic Chinese populations, such as Thailand, Singapore, Malaysia, and Indonesia. Confucianism has played a central role in shaping East Asian cultures and, to some extent, other parts of Asia.

The fifth cultural dimension, Long-Term Orientation (LTO), was introduced by Hofstede (1991) in response to concerns that the original four-dimension framework

[7] As reported in Tables 1 and 4, of all of the countries examined around the world, the East Asian, or Confucian countries/territories were found to have the highest (lowest) average scores for LTO (UA). We identify a country characterized by Confucius Temples as a 'Confucian territory', with such territories in our sample being identified as China, Hong Kong, Indonesia, Japan, South Korea, Malaysia, Singapore, Thailand and Vietnam. The countries within the Confucian territories are the same as those defined as being in East Asia, with the one exception of the Philippines. Since the common cultural value in the East Asian countries is characterized mainly by LTO, UA and IVR, we focus our discussion on these three cultural dimensions, and ignore the other three measures.

may have been biased toward Western cultural values. Based on the Chinese Value Survey (CVS) conducted in 1971, a long-term–oriented culture (high LTO), initially referred to as "Confucian dynamism," was found to be associated with values prevalent in Confucian-influenced societies, such as patience, persistence, thrift, and a long-term commitment to future-oriented goals. This mindset encourages present effort and investment in education as preparation for the future (Hofstede, 1991; Hofstede, Hofstede, and Minkov, 2010). In contrast, individuals in short-term–oriented cultures (low LTO) tend to emphasize immediate outcomes and place greater weight on the past and present rather than the future.

When applied to our context, individuals in a long-term–oriented culture are more willing to forgo current consumption and exhibit a stronger propensity to save in order to obtain greater returns in the future. In contrast, individuals in a short-term–oriented culture tend to place greater emphasis on current consumption. We therefore argue that LTO scores can help explain the high saving rates observed in long-term–oriented countries, such as those in East Asia, as well as the low saving rates in short-term–oriented countries, such as those in Africa and Latin America.[8]

As noted by Hofstede (2001), the Uncertainty Avoidance (UA) index captures the extent to which members of a society feel uncomfortable with uncertainty or ambiguous situations. Intuitively, a high (low) UA index may be associated with greater risk aversion (risk tolerance).[9] In a high-uncertainty-avoidance culture, individuals are less tolerant of uncertain or unknown situations and tend to take immediate action to reduce ambiguity, hedge against risks, or seek additional compensation. In contrast, in a low-uncertainty-avoidance culture, individuals are generally more tolerant of ambiguity and uncertainty and are more willing to take risks.

Li and Zahra (2012) note that, in venture capital activities, managers with a lower propensity for uncertainty avoidance tend to be more comfortable with the unpredictability and ambiguity inherent in innovative projects, for which established rules or precedents may not exist. Conversely, managers with high uncertainty

---

[8] The LTO measure was also found to be positively correlated with economic growth in Hofstede and Bond (1988), Franke, Hofstede and Bond (1991) and Yeh and Lawrence (1995).

[9] It is important to distinguish between UA and risk avoidance. As emphasized by Hofstede (2001, p.148) 'Uncertainty avoidance does not equate to risk avoidance'. Individuals are said to be *risk averse* if they are unwilling to accept or are indifferent to any fair game; in other words, individuals are more risk averse if they are more hesitant to take on risk than others. Relatively, an individual in a *high uncertainty avoidance* (high UA) culture will tend to take immediate action to reduce any potential risk, whereas, in contrast, an individual in a *low uncertainty avoidance* (low UA) culture may be quite readily prepared to take risk. Rieger, Wang and Hens (2015) carried out a large-scale international survey on risk attitudes in 53 countries, with their results showing that risk attitudes in the sample countries were dependent not only on economic conditions, but also on cultural factors, as measured by individualism and the UA in the Hofstede dimensions. Their findings indicated that UA corresponded to greater risk aversion in the domain of 'gains', and greater acceptance of risk in the domain of 'losses'. They computed the 'relative risk premium' (RRP) to measure risk aversion (if it was positive) and risk acceptance (if it was negative). Their results, reported in Table 5, also showed that for the 53 countries, the respective correlations between UA and risk aversion (a positive RRP) and risk acceptance (a negative RRP) were 0.088 and -0.059. Readers can refer to Rieger et al. (2015) for discussions on the relationship between uncertainty avoidance and risk avoidance.

avoidance are more likely to experience anxiety in uncertain environments and may either avoid innovative projects or require a higher risk premium.

Several studies have suggested that private saving behavior can be influenced by shocks, such as income uncertainty and financial crises.[10] On the one hand, individuals in high-uncertainty-avoidance societies, such as those in parts of Latin America, may be less tolerant of potential future income reductions and therefore reduce current saving in order to maintain their usual level of consumption. On the other hand, individuals in low-uncertainty-avoidance societies, such as those in East Asia, may be more accustomed to uncertainty and ambiguity and thus more willing to reduce consumption in order to maintain their usual level of saving—or even increase saving as a precautionary measure.[11]

Hofstede et al. (2010) introduced the sixth cultural dimension, Indulgence versus Restraint (IVR), to describe how societies regulate the gratification of basic human desires. The IVR dimension helps explain cross-cultural differences in attitudes toward enjoyment, happiness, work–life balance, and broader patterns of social behavior.

"Indulgence" refers to cultures that allow relatively free gratification of basic human desires related to enjoying life and having fun. People in indulgent societies tend to value leisure, personal freedom, optimism, and emotional expression. They are also more likely to believe that they have control over their own happiness. In contrast, "Restraint" characterizes cultures that regulate gratification through strict social norms. In restrained societies, individuals are more inclined to control their desires, emphasize duty over leisure, and perceive life outcomes as being shaped by external rules or obligations.

Hofstede et al. (2010) show that indulgent societies tend to be short-term oriented, more comfortable with discretionary spending, exhibit lower levels of self-discipline, and place less emphasis on thrift. In terms of saving behavior, indulgence (high IVR) and Short-Term Orientation (STO) reflect similar attitudes, both of which contrast sharply with the values associated with Long-Term Orientation (LTO).

Based on the foregoing discussion, we hypothesize that private saving behavior in East Asian countries is influenced by Confucianism, high LTO, and low UA. For a

[10] Examples include Leland (1968), Mody et al. (2012), Bande and Riveiro (2013) and Levenko (2020). In a pioneering article, Leland (1968) showed that the precautionary demand for saving was a positive function of uncertainty; in other words, the level of additional saving becomes higher as future income becomes more uncertain, in terms of a given expected value. More importantly, as emphasized by Leland (1968), not only does uncertainty itself potentially influence the level of precautionary saving, but the degree of tolerance for uncertainty also affects the level of demand for precautionary saving.

[11] Chamon, Liu and Prasad (2013) examined a 1989-2000 panel of urban Chinese households, calibrating a buffer-stock savings model to obtain quantitative estimates on the impact of rising household-specific income uncertainty, as well as an additional shock to household income, the pension reforms introduced in the late 1990s. Their calibrations suggested that rising income uncertainty and the pension reforms had led to both younger and older households significantly raising their saving rates.

given East Asian country, Confucian norms combined with a high LTO are expected to promote higher private saving rates, while a low UA helps explain the persistence of such high saving rates, even during periods of financial crisis. Empirical evidence supporting this perspective is presented in the subsequent sections.

Our research makes at least five major contributions to the literature. First, using pooled regression models under both unconditional and conditional specifications, we find that high LTO is associated with high private saving rates, while low UA helps explain the persistence of elevated private saving behavior across countries. The inclusion of the cultural proxies LTO and UA jointly increases the regression R^2 by 13.2 percentage points. We therefore argue that the strong persistence of high private saving rates in China, Japan, and other East Asian countries is largely attributable to their cultural attributes of high LTO and low UA. We further find that countries in which Confucianism is culturally embedded exhibit a greater propensity for private saving.

Second, prior studies suggest that credible evidence on the cultural determinants of saving behavior requires addressing the challenges of measuring culture, limited data availability, and potential endogeneity. In this study, we address these concerns by employing all six measurable cultural dimensions proposed by Hofstede as proxies for national culture. Specifically, we use LTO data for 84 countries; UA, IND, PD, and MAS data for 61 countries; and IVR data for 82 countries. We combine these measures with the largest currently available panel dataset on private saving rates.

Third, to address potential endogeneity between culture and saving, Ye et al. (2020) employ two-stage least squares (2SLS) estimation and use an English-language dummy as an instrument for all cultural variables. In contrast, we use more targeted instruments. Specifically, we employ genetic distance and linguistic distance as instruments for LTO, and two religion-based variables—hierarchical religion and Protestantism—as instruments for UA (discussed in detail below). According to Nash and Patel (2019), these instruments are more appropriate because they are widely recognized in the culture-and-finance literature.

Fourth, our results further indicate that the IVR measure exerts a negative, albeit relatively weak, influence on private saving rates worldwide at the 5% level of significance. In strongly restrained societies (low IVR), individuals tend to adhere closely to social norms and are bound by strict behavioral expectations (Hofstede, 2010). This suggests that individuals in self-restrained cultures are more likely to constrain their consumption, thereby contributing to higher private saving rates.

Given that individuals in the "other Asian countries" are predominantly adherents of hierarchical religions (Islam, Judaism, and Eastern Orthodoxy)[12] and that this group exhibits the lowest average IVR scores among all regions, our findings may help explain why these countries have the second-highest average private saving rates[13]. In contrast, South America has the highest average IVR score, which may help explain why it exhibits the lower average private saving rate.

Fifth, we find that cultural indulgence (high IVR) combined with a short-term orientation (low LTO) helps explain why Africa has the lowest private saving rate, while South America ranks second lowest.

Although our findings are robust to potential endogeneity concerns, we conduct additional robustness checks and employ an instrumental variable (IV) approach to ensure that our results are not driven by omitted demographic variables, potential simultaneity, or measurement error in the cultural proxies.

The remainder of this paper is organized as follows. Section 2 introduces Confucianism and Hofstede's cultural dimensions. Section 3 reviews the related literature on how economic behavior is influenced by cultures characterized by LTO, UA, and IVR, and develops the corresponding hypotheses. Section 4 presents the baseline regression model. Section 5 describes the data, reports the empirical results, and tests the hypotheses. Section 6 extends the model, conducts robustness checks, and addresses concerns regarding potential endogeneity. Finally, Section 7 concludes.

---

[12] Hierarchical religions are religions with a clear leadership system and ranked authority (such as popes, patriarchs, bishops, or prophets). These religions have organized leadership and centralized authority structures.

[13] As listed in Table 1, the 'other Asian countries' include Armenia, Azerbaijan, Bangladesh, India, Iran, Israel, Jordan, Kyrgyz Republic, Pakistan, Saudi Arabia, and Turkey.

2. CONFUCIANISM AND HOFSTEDE'S CULTURAL DIMENSIONS

2.1 Confucianism

Confucianism is a major philosophical tradition in Chinese history, based on the teachings of Confucius (551–479 BCE), one of China's most influential philosophers. Rather than being primarily a religion, Confucianism is a system of ethical and social thought that emphasizes moral cultivation, social harmony, and proper human relationships.

A central principle of Confucianism is that social harmony originates from individual moral self-cultivation. Confucius argued that individuals must first refine their own character; when people behave morally, families become stable and society becomes orderly.

One of the core concepts in Confucianism is Ren (仁), commonly translated as benevolence or humaneness. Ren refers to compassion, empathy, and concern for others. It represents the highest moral virtue and guides interpersonal conduct.

Another essential concept is Li (礼), meaning ritual, propriety, or proper conduct. Li encompasses social norms, etiquette, and traditional practices. Through adherence to Li, individuals maintain respect, hierarchy, and social order.

Yi (义), or righteousness, emphasizes acting in accordance with moral principles rather than personal gain. A Confucian individual is expected to choose what is morally right, even when doing so entails personal sacrifice.

Confucianism also places strong emphasis on Xiao (孝), or filial piety, which denotes respect, obedience, and duty toward parents and elders. Confucius regarded the family as the foundation of society, with harmonious family relationships serving as the basis for social stability.

Confucianism has exerted a profound and enduring influence on East Asian countries, particularly China. Its principles have shaped traditional education systems, family structures, governance philosophies, and social norms. Many of its values continue to influence contemporary East Asian societies.

2.2 Hofstede's Cultural Dimensions

Hofstede's Culture's Consequences (1980, 1991, 2001, 2005) is one of the most influential works in cross-cultural psychology and has been widely cited in marketing, management, international business, and, more recently, finance. The cultural dimensions were derived from surveys of approximately 117,000 IBM employees across more than 50 countries conducted between 1967 and 1973.

The survey included 60 core questions and an additional 66 recommended questions covering four broad categories: employee satisfaction, perceptions, personal goals and beliefs, and demographics. After data screening and stratification across job classifications, 40 countries were retained with sufficient data for analysis. Analysis of variance (ANOVA) was used to assess the relative contributions of country, occupation, gender, and age to the observed variance. Subsequently, factor analysis was employed to extract cultural indices.

Hofstede's survey-based research identifies six primary dimensions of national culture:

1. **Uncertainty Avoidance (UA)**

   UA measures the degree to which members of a society feel uncomfortable with uncertainty and ambiguity. A high (low) UA score indicates that individuals tend to avoid (accept) uncertain and unstructured situations.

2. **Individualism (IND) versus Collectivism**

   High IND reflects a society in which individuals are loosely connected and prioritize personal interests and those of their immediate families. Low IND (Collectivism) indicates a collectivist society, where individuals emphasize group interests, social harmony, and close interpersonal ties.

3. **Power Distance (PD)**

   PD measures the extent to which inequality in power and hierarchical order is accepted within a society. In high-PD societies, individuals are more likely to accept authority, status differences, and unequal power distributions, and may be reluctant to challenge superiors. In low-PD societies, individuals are less tolerant of hierarchical inequality and more willing to express disagreement with authority.

4. **Masculinity (MAS) versus Femininity**

   High MAS indicates a societal preference for achievement, assertiveness, competition, and material success. Low MAS (Femininity) reflects a preference for cooperation, modesty, caring for others, and quality of life.

5. **Long-Term Orientation (LTO) versus Short-Term Orientation**

   High LTO reflects a cultural emphasis on future-oriented values such as persistence, thrift, patience, and long-term commitment—values often associated with Confucian traditions. In contrast, low LTO (Short-term orientation) emphasizes respect for tradition, fulfilling social obligations, and short-term outcomes.

6. **Indulgence versus Restraint (IVR)**

   High IVR (Indulgence) indicates that a society allows relatively free gratification of basic human desires related to enjoyment and leisure. Low IVR (Restraint) characterizes societies in which gratification is regulated by strict social norms, and individuals are expected to exercise self-control and conform to social expectations.

The scores for Hofstede's six cultural dimensions are based on aggregated survey responses from each country. Statistical techniques, such as factor analysis, are used to identify systematic patterns in the responses. Country-level averages are then standardized and converted into index scores, typically ranging from 0 to 100.

2.3 The Relationship between Confucianism and Hofstede's Cultural Dimensions

Among Hofstede's six cultural dimensions, three are particularly related to Confucian thought: Long-Term Orientation (LTO), Uncertainty Avoidance (UA), and Indulgence versus Restraint (IVR).

Long-Term Orientation (LTO) is the dimension most closely associated with Confucianism. Its development was initially inspired by cross-cultural research in Asia conducted by Michael Harris Bond, who created the Chinese Value Survey (CVS)[14] to better capture East Asian cultural values that were not fully reflected in Hofstede's original framework.[15]

The LTO score is derived primarily from responses to standardized survey instruments administered through large-scale cross-national research programs. The surveys were initially conducted with IBM employees and later expanded using additional international datasets. The questionnaire items were designed to capture

[14] The Chinese Value Survey (CVS) is a research questionnaire developed in the 1980s to measure cultural values rooted in Chinese philosophy and society. It was created by the Chinese Culture Connection group to better understand values that were not fully captured in Western-based surveys, such as those developed by Geert Hofstede.

[15] When Geert Hofstede added Michael Harris Bond's research to his framework, he introduced a fifth dimension called "Confucian Dynamism." However, scholars later found the name misleading. The values it describes are not limited to Confucian societies, and many non-Confucian cultures also show strong long-term orientation. The dimension focuses more broadly on perseverance and planning for the future rather than Confucianism itself. As a result, it was renamed "Long-Term Orientation," a more neutral term that reflects its cross-cultural relevance.

cultural values associated with:

- Future-oriented thinking, including perseverance, thrift, and long-term planning
- Respect for tradition versus openness to adaptation and change
- Delayed gratification versus preference for immediate results
- Pragmatic orientation versus normative (rule-based and tradition-centered) thinking

Typical survey items ask respondents to evaluate the importance of values such as persistence, saving and thrift, respect for tradition, and personal stability. Country-level mean scores are standardized and transformed into an index typically ranging from 0 to 100. Higher LTO scores indicate a cultural orientation that emphasizes long-term goals, adaptability, pragmatism, and sustained effort, while lower scores reflect a stronger focus on short-term outcomes, adherence to tradition, fulfillment of social obligations, and maintenance of established norms.

Uncertainty Avoidance (UA) and Confucian thought are related but distinct constructs. Confucianism emphasizes social harmony, hierarchical roles, ritual propriety (Li), and moral self-cultivation, all of which contribute to predictability and social order. In this sense, Confucian societies may appear similar to high-UA cultures, which value structure and stability. For instance, using stock transaction records from individual investors at a large Chinese brokerage, Hao et al. (2024) found a significant negative relationship between Confucianism and lottery-type stock preferences, suggesting that Confucian culture discourages speculative or high-risk investment behaviors.

However, as will be shown in Section 4, the UA values of Confucian-influenced countries are relatively low, indicating a culture that exhibits tolerance for uncertainty. This finding appears to contradict the expectation that Confucian societies would align with high UA.

The UA index was developed from IBM survey data collected across more than 50 countries between 1967 and 1973. Hofstede applied factor analysis to identify clusters of items reflecting attitudes toward ambiguity, rule orientation, job security, and work-related stress. Items that loaded strongly on the same factor were interpreted as representing a shared societal approach to uncertainty. The model was later refined and expanded with additional data, especially through collaborations with Michael Minkov. National mean scores were standardized and aggregated into an index typically ranging from 0 to 100, with higher scores indicating stronger preferences for formal rules, structured environments, and predictability, and lower scores indicating tolerance for ambiguity and flexibility.

Indulgence versus Restraint (IVR) is also closely related to Confucianism. Confucian thought emphasizes self-discipline, moderation, and prioritizing societal duties over personal desires, which aligns with low IVR, or societal restraint. IVR was incorporated into Hofstede's model at a later stage based on data from the World Values Survey (WVS)[16], rather than the earlier IBM surveys. Factor analysis of the WVS identified clusters of items reflecting life enjoyment, subjective well-being, perceived control over life, and attitudes toward leisure and gratification. Items loading strongly on a common factor were interpreted as representing an underlying cultural orientation toward indulgence versus restraint.

Country-level mean scores were standardized and aggregated into an index, typically ranging from 0 to 100. Higher IVR scores indicate cultures that permit relatively free gratification of basic human desires and emphasize enjoyment and leisure, whereas lower IVR scores indicate stronger social regulation and suppression of gratification through adherence to norms.

---

[16] The World Values Survey (WVS) is a large international research project that studies people's values, beliefs, and attitudes across different countries. It was launched in 1981 by sociologist Ronald Inglehart and involves researchers from around the world.

3. LITERATURE REVIEW AND HYPOTHESIS DEVELOPMENT

3.1 Long-term Orientation (LTO)

As discussed earlier, cultures with a long-term orientation (LTO) are generally characterized by values associated with Confucian teachings, including patience, persistence, thrift, future orientation, and a concern for reputation. Hofstede (2001) argued that these personal virtues within LTO cultures significantly influence business decisions and investor behavior. Subsequent research has also demonstrated that long-term oriented cultures affect various financial and corporate outcomes, including cash holdings (Chang and Noorbakhsh, 2009; Orlova, Rao, and Kang, 2017), mergers and acquisitions (Ferris, Jayaraman, and Sabherwal, 2013), IPO underpricing (Costa, Crawford, and Jakob, 2013), leverage decisions (Wang and Esqueda, 2014; Haq, Hu, Faff, and Pathan, 2018), hedging behavior (Lievenbruck and Schmid, 2014), stock market herding (Chang and Lin, 2015), and sovereign credit ratings (Dang and Partington, 2020).

In countries with higher LTO scores, investment opportunities are generally evaluated based on their potential for long-term value creation. Business managers in these cultures tend to forgo short-term returns in favor of strategies that enhance long-term profitability and firm value.

For example, Chang and Noorbakhsh (2009) analyzed financial data from diverse industries in 45 countries during 1995–2004, yielding more than 75,000 firm-year observations. They found that managers in long-term oriented countries exhibited a more stable and cautious outlook, resulting in higher cash holdings and greater liquidity.

Ferris et al. (2013) examined the role of CEO overconfidence in international M&A activity from 2000 to 2006, using a sample of CEOs from Fortune Global 500 firms. They found that overconfident CEOs were more likely to engage in riskier or non-diversifying acquisitions, financed with cash. Importantly, CEOs in countries with lower LTO scores exhibited greater overconfidence, whereas high-LTO cultures promoted more measured decision-making.

Similarly, Costa, Crawford, and Jakob (2013) investigated the impact of national culture on IPO underpricing across 39 countries. They found that managers in high-LTO countries tended to pursue IPO strategies that favored the long-term benefits of the firm. High LTO scores were positively associated with greater IPO underpricing, as managers were willing to accept short-term losses to secure the capital necessary to achieve long-term objectives.

Wang and Esqueda (2014) investigated the effects of national culture on firm capital structure decisions using a 1996–2010 sample of 621 emerging-market ADRs from 23 countries. Their results indicated that national cultural characteristics partially explained firms' capital structure choices, with firms from high-LTO countries tending to rely less on debt. Similarly, Haq et al. (2018), analyzing a 2000–2013 sample of 1,701 banks across 79 countries, found that banks in high-LTO countries were generally less leveraged.

Lievenbruck and Schmid (2014) examined a 2000–2009 sample of at least 500 energy utility firms from over 50 countries to assess whether national culture directly influences hedging behavior. They found a strong negative relationship between LTO scores and hedging: both the likelihood of hedging and the volume hedged were lower in high-LTO cultures. The authors argued that firms in short-term oriented countries were more impatient for immediate outcomes and thus preferred short-term gains that could be secured through hedging.

Chang and Lin (2015) explored the impact of national culture on investor herding behavior in international stock markets. Their results showed that significant herding was observed in only 18 of the 50 markets studied. However, herding behavior was more prevalent in high-LTO markets and in markets with lower levels of investor sophistication. They suggested that investors in Confucian-influenced markets tend to emphasize public morality and follow the majority, reflecting long-term oriented cultural values.

Finally, Dang and Partington (2020) analyzed sovereign credit ratings using Standard & Poor's data from 1975–2013 covering 77 countries, and Moody's ratings from 1974–2013 covering 72 countries. Their findings revealed that both the levels and changes in sovereign credit ratings could be significantly explained by national culture, with long-term oriented cultures associated with higher sovereign ratings.

3.2 Uncertainty Avoidance (UA)

As noted in Section 1, the Uncertainty Avoidance (UA) dimension reflects the extent to which individuals feel comfortable in situations with uncertain outcomes and their willingness to confront risk. In other words, UA captures the degree to which a society tolerates ambiguity. While it may be intuitive to equate high UA with risk aversion and low UA with risk seeking, Hofstede (2001) emphasized that "uncertainty avoidance does not equal risk aversion." Nevertheless, empirical evidence often shows that individuals from high-UA countries tend to behave more conservatively, while those from low-UA countries are relatively more willing to accept risk.

For example, Kwok and Tadesse (2006) examined how UA affects investment preferences and found that countries with higher UA scores tend to have relatively risk-averse, bank-based financial systems, whereas countries with lower UA scores favor market-based financial systems. Chui and Kwok (2008) reported that higher-UA countries exhibit greater life insurance consumption, suggesting a stronger preference for precautionary measures. Similarly, Bova and Vance (2019) found that employees from high-UA countries tend to exercise stock options earlier and place less value on option-based compensation, indicating heightened risk aversion. These results imply that UA influences both the costs and benefits for firms offering employee stock options (ESOs).

At the corporate level, Li, Griffin, Yue, and Zhao (2013) used firm-level data from 35 countries and identified a negative association between UA and corporate risk-taking, showing that national culture affects corporate behavior through both formal institutions and managerial decision-making. Chen, Dou, Rhee, Truong, and Veeraghavan (2015), analyzing 27,801 firms across 41 countries from 1989 to 2009, found a positive relationship between UA and corporate cash holdings, suggesting that high-UA cultures encourage precautionary cash reserves. Similarly, banks in high-UA countries tend to assume less risk, which contributed to superior performance during the financial crisis (Kanagaretnam, Lim, and Lobo, 2014; Boubakri, Mirzaei, and Samet, 2017).

UA also affects individual investor behavior. Tan, Cheong, and Zurbruegg (2019) analyzed trading histories from 21 countries and demonstrated that investors from lower-UA cultures tend to exhibit risk-taking behaviors: they trade larger volumes and allotments, trade more frequently, and take on greater exposure. Conversely, investors from higher-UA cultures are more risk-averse, trading smaller volumes and acting cautiously.

Overall, the literature suggests that UA influences both corporate and individual financial behavior, shaping risk preferences, precautionary actions, and the overall approach to uncertainty in economic decision-making.

Finally, uncertainty avoidance can also help explain cross-country differences in the maturity structure of corporate debt. Using firm-year data from 40 countries over the 1991–2006 period, Zheng, Ghoul, Guedhami, and Kwok (2012) found that firms in high-UA countries tended to rely more on short-term debt, whereas firms in low-UA countries preferred long-term debt. This evidence further highlights the influence of UA on financial decision-making at both the individual and corporate levels.

Based on the preceding discussion and the literature reviewed in Section 1, we propose four related hypotheses, with the first two linked to Hofstede's LTO and UA measures:

Hypothesis 1. *Individuals in long-term (short-term) oriented cultures will tend to have higher (lower) private saving rates.*

Hypothesis 2. *Individuals in low (high) uncertainty avoidance countries will tend to have higher (lower) private saving rates; when faced with potential income reductions, those from low (high) UA countries will tend to retain (reduce) their normal level of saving.*

Hypothesis 1 implies that the high LTO levels in East Asian countries largely determine their elevated private saving rates, while Hypothesis 2 suggests that low UA levels contribute to the persistence of these high saving rates. Since Confucianism represents the common cultural core of China, Japan, and other East Asian countries, we propose a third hypothesis:

Hypothesis 3. *Countries with Confucian cultural norms will tend to exhibit higher private saving behavior.*

These hypotheses collectively provide a theoretical framework linking cultural dimensions to private saving behavior across countries, particularly emphasizing the unique financial patterns observed in East Asia.

3.3 Indulgence versus Restraint (IVR)

As described in Section 2, the Indulgence versus Restraint (IVR) dimension captures the degree to which societies allow the gratification of basic and natural human desires. The indulgence pole refers to "the tendency to allow relatively free gratification of basic and natural human desires related to enjoying life and having fun," whereas the restraint pole reflects "a conviction that such gratification should be curbed and regulated by strict social norms" (Hofstede et al., 2010).

Hofstede et al. (2010) show that indulgent societies tend to be short-term oriented, more comfortable with discretionary spending, exhibit lower self-control, and place little emphasis on thrift. In contrast, societies on the restraint pole are guided by strong social rules and norms, which individuals feel obliged to follow, emphasizing moderation and duty over immediate gratification.

Several studies highlight the impact of IVR on financial behavior. Alipour and Yaprak (2024) examined the influence of IVR on firms' cash holdings across 39 countries and found that firms in indulgent societies tend to hold higher cash levels due to a combination of greater risk-taking (precautionary motive) and weaker moral constraints on managers (agency motive). Similarly, Alipour and Yaprak (2022) demonstrated that firms in indulgent societies exhibit higher risk-taking behaviors due to less rigid structures and a greater inclination to discount potential losses.

At the individual level, Hofstede et al. (2010) note that people in highly self-restrained societies (low IVR) tend to respect social norms and adhere to strict regulations, limiting consumption and, as a result, contributing to higher private saving rates.

Based on the above discussion, an indulgent culture (high IVR) is expected to be associated with lower levels of private saving, whereas a restrained culture (low IVR) is expected to encourage higher private saving. Accordingly, we propose the following hypothesis:

Hypothesis 4. *Individuals in societies characterized by high indulgence (high IVR) tend to exhibit lower private saving rates, whereas individuals in societies characterized by high restraint (low IVR) tend to exhibit higher private saving rates.*

4. BASELINE REGRESSION

To examine the effects of Hofstede's cultural dimensions on private saving rates within a regression framework, we estimate the following baseline model:

$$Private\_Saving\_Rate_{it} = \alpha + \beta CulturalProxy_i + \gamma Control_{it} + \varphi_t + \varepsilon_{it} \quad (1)$$

where i and t denote country and year, respectively. The cultural dimension scores—Long-Term Orientation (LTO), Uncertainty Avoidance (UA), Masculinity (MAS), Individualism (IND), Power Distance (PD), and Indulgence versus Restraint (IVR) (Hofstede et al., 2010)—serve as the cultural proxies. Control represents a vector of country-level characteristics (discussed below), ϕ_t denotes year fixed effects, and ε_{it} is the error term.

Consistent with the mainstream approach adopted in much of the cultural economics literature, we estimate pooled ordinary least squares (OLS) regressions including year fixed effects. Robust standard errors clustered at the country level are employed to account for potential heteroskedasticity and serial correlation within countries.[17]

Our key variable of interest is CulturalProxy. A positive (negative) and statistically significant coefficient βwould provide support for the hypothesized positive (negative) relationship between the respective cultural dimension and private saving behavior.

The control variables included in the baseline specification are motivated by traditional consumption theory and prior empirical research. For comparability, we follow the specifications used by Loayza et al. (2000) and Grigoli et al. (2018). Specifically, we include:

- The logarithm of real gross private disposable income (GPDI) per capita
- The real growth rate of per capita GPDI

[17] As described in various Econometrics textbooks (e.g. Asterious and Hall, 2011), *country fixed effects* cannot be estimated when the explained variables (cultural proxies) in a regression remain constant over time. Instead, we have included two additional country-specific time-invariant variables, the Underdevelopment Index (UI) and the Political and Governance Environment Composite (PGEC), as exogenous variables in the baseline regression. The UI for a country is the sum of its rankings on infant mortality, internet users per population, literacy, unemployment rate and paved airport runways, details of which are obtained from the World Bank. The PGEC for a country is the sum of its rankings on Voice of the People, Political Stability, Government Effectiveness, Regulatory Quality, Rule of Law and Corruption Control, with these variables being obtained from Kaufmann, Kraay and Mastruzzi (2003). A higher value for UI indicates better development, whilst a higher value for PGEC indicates that a country has a more stable political system and a higher quality of governance mechanism. If these country-specific time-invariant variables are controlled, the estimated coefficients on the cultural aspects are more likely to indicate a pure culture effect. Based upon the lack of availability of data, we have reduced the number of the sample countries in the present study from 84 to 64 for LTO, from 61 to 54 for IND, UA, PD and MAS, and from 82 to 62 for IVR. The results obtained from the inclusion of the two additional country-specific variables reveal that for all of the variables of concern in Table 5, the signs and significance remain unchanged. For space-saving considerations, the results are not reported but are available upon request.

- The inflation rate
- The real deposit interest rate
- Private sector credit as a percentage of GPDI
- The logarithm of the terms of trade
- The old-age dependency ratio
- The share of the urban population

These variables control for income levels, macroeconomic stability, financial development, demographic structure, and structural economic characteristics that may influence private saving behavior.

5. DATA AND HYPOTHESIS TESTING

5.1 Data Description

The private saving rate used in this study is defined as *gross private saving* (GPS) scaled by *gross private disposable income* (GPDI). This measure can be decomposed into the sum of the household saving rate and the corporate saving rate.

We construct a comprehensive and up-to-date panel dataset on global saving behavior, following the approach of Grigoli et al., who emphasize the necessity of combining data from multiple international sources.[18] Accordingly, our private saving data are obtained from the International Monetary Fund World Economic Outlook (WEO) database, the United Nations National Accounts (UNNA) database, and the World Bank Saving database.[19]

The control variables are collected from eight different international databases to ensure consistency and broad country coverage. The resulting panel comprises an unbalanced dataset covering 165 countries over the period 1981–2012, making it one of the most extensive macroeconomic datasets currently available on saving aggregates and related determinants. As the dataset is unbalanced, the number of time-series observations varies across countries due to differences in data availability.

The cultural dimension scores—Long-Term Orientation (LTO), Uncertainty Avoidance (UA), Masculinity (MAS), Individualism (IND), Power Distance (PD), and Indulgence versus Restraint (IVR)[20]—are drawn from Hofstede et al. (2010). These indices are standardized on a 0–100 scale. Since cultural scores are time-invariant at the country level, they are matched with the macroeconomic panel covering the 1981–2012 sample period.

After merging the private saving data with Hofstede's cultural indicators, the effective sample sizes vary by dimension due to data availability. Specifically, we

---

[18] We are grateful to Alexander Herman for kindly providing us with data on world savings, as well as other related variables.

[19] The data sources were: IMF Financial statistics, Haver Analytics, the IMF WEO, the World bank World Development Indicators, the Bank of International Settlements database, the Quinn Index database, the Standardized World Income Inequality database and the IMF Fiscal Monitor database.

[20] The four original dimensions, IND, UA, PD and MAS, are derived from the empirical works of Hofstede carried out between 1967 and 1973. In Hofstede and Hofstede (2005) (Hofstede et al. (2010)), Hofstede not only updated the scores of the four (five) original cultural dimensions, but also proposed an additional cultural dimension, LTO (IVR). Tang and Koveos (2008) argued that changes in economic conditions were the source of cultural dynamics, whilst the endurance of the institutional characteristics (such as religion, language, legal system and ethnic heterogeneity) provides the foundation for cultural stability. Beugelsdijk, Maseland and Van Hoorn (2015) have tested whether the country scored on the Hofstede dimensions of national culture have changed over the past decades and whether changes in these scores invalidate the continued use of earlier surveys by Hofstede. They found that cultural changes are absolute rather than relative, meaning that the differences in cultural scores on the Hofstede dimensions between country pairs are generally stable.

obtain:

- 84 countries with available LTO scores
- 61 countries with UA, MAS, IND, and PD scores
- 82 countries with IVR scores

Table 1 reports the means and standard deviations of private saving rates and the six cultural dimensions for the full sample period, disaggregated by regional groupings: Confucian territory, East Asia, Other Asia, Africa, Europe, North America, Latin America, and the Pacific region.[21]

Table 1 Summary statistics for private saving rates and Hofstede's cultural dimensions by country and country groups

This table reports sample periods, country and country-group averages of private saving rates (for 84 countries), country scores and country-group average scores of Hofstede's (2010) six culture dimensions – LTO (on 84 countries), UA, MAS, IND, PD (on 61 countries), and IVR (on 82 countries).

Country	*Sample Period*	*Average Private saving rate*	*LTO*	*UA*	*MAS*	*IND*	*PD*	*IVR*
Confucian Territory		**33.08 (7.93)**	**67.51 (22.16)**	**48.98 (28.10)**	**52.78 (17.50)**	**23.22 (8.71)**	**72.44 (13.66)**	**40.22 (14.03)**
China	1990-2012	49.24(5.19)	87	30	66	20	80	24
Hong Kong	1990-2012	31.71(1.98)	61	29	57	25	68	17
Indonesia	1988-2012	27.24(4.98)	62	48	46	14	78	38
Japan	1981-2012	30.06(2.19)	88	92	95	46	54	42
Malaysia	1981-2012	29.36(5.06)	41	36	50	26	104	57
Singapore	1981-2012	41.61(5.06)	72	8	48	20	74	46
South Korea	1981-2012	31.73(4.23)	100	85	39	18	60	63
Thailand	1985-2012	28.96(2.27)	32	64	34	20	64	45
Vietnam	1997-2012	26.42(3.26)	57	30	40	20	70	30
East Asia		***31.62 (8.55)***	***62.76 (24.57)***	***48.40 (26.44)***	***53.90 (16.94)***	***24.10 (8.68)***	***74.60 (14.48)***	***40.40 (13.32)***
China	1990-2012	49.24(5.19)	87	30	66	20	80	24
Hong Kong	1990-2012	31.71(1.98)	61	29	57	25	68	17
Indonesia	1988-2012	27.24(4.98)	62	48	46	14	78	38
Japan	1981-2012	30.06(2.19)	88	92	95	46	54	42
Malaysia	1981-2012	29.36(5.06)	41	36	50	26	104	57

[21] As presented in Table 1, the Confucian cultural sphere comprises China, Hong Kong, Indonesia, Japan, Malaysia, Singapore, South Korea, Thailand, and Vietnam, as elaborated in Section 4.5.

Philippines	1981-2012	20.61(3.55)	27	44	64	32	94	42
Singapore	1981-2012	41.61(5.06)	72	8	48	20	74	46
South Korea	1981-2012	31.73(4.23)	100	85	39	18	60	63
Thailand	1985-2012	28.96(2.27)	32	64	34	20	64	45
Vietnam	1997-2012	26.42(3.26)	57	30	40	20	70	30
Other Asia		***26.27 (11.69)***	***40.90 (16.37)***	***66.20 (13.42)***	***49.33 (4.85)***	***35.67 (14.34)***	***58.17 (22.15)***	***32.33 (15.73)***
Armenia	1996-2012	14.25(9.56)	61					
Azerbaijan	1999-2012	34.46(13.37)	61					22
Bangladesh	1981-2012	20.58(4.01)	47	60	55	20	80	20
India	2002-2012	33.85(2.28)	51	40	56	48	77	26
Iran	1991-2012	40.41(7.80)	14	59	43	41	58	40
Israel	1986-2011	26.68(3.54)	38	81	47	54	13	
Jordan	1990-2012	22.03(7.03)	16					43
Kyrgyz Rep	1998-2007	16.95(8.58)	66					39
Pakistan	2004-2012	15.78(1.54)	50	70	50	14	55	0
Saudi Arabia	1991-2012	37.22(12.20)	36					52
Turkey	2003-2012	16.79(4.39)	46	85	45	37	66	49
Africa		***16.98 (12.96)***	***20.33 (10.14)***					***44.30 (23.05)***
Algeria	1990-2012	45.99(8.51)	26					32
Burkina Faso	1981-2012	6.49(5.98)	27					18
Egypt	1987-2012	21.90(5.46)	7					4
Ghana	1982-2012	11.02(6.31)	4					72
Mali	1992-2012	18.11(6.18)	20					43
Nigeria	1981-2012	18.71(14.88)	13					84
Rwanda	1982-2005	8.36(3.80)	18					37
South Africa	1981-2012	20.27(3.72)	34					63
Tanzania	1995-2012	8.92(5.59)	34					38
Uganda	1984-2012	9.63(3.14)	24					52
Europe		***24.42 (7.71)***	***54.95 (18.60)***	***69.19 (24.50)***	***45.69 (24.40)***	***57.19 (17.75)***	***53.34 (22.05)***	***40.54 (19.59)***
Albania	1996-2012	18.78(3.67)	61					15
Austria	1981-2013	28.88(1.40)	60	70	79	55	11	63
Belgium	1981-2013	31.08(1.97)	82	94	54	75	65	57
Bosnia	2000-2012	7.30(3.79)	70					44
Bulgaria	1998-2012	14.22(6.52)	69	85	40	30	70	16
Croatia	1995-2012	22.58(4.99)	58	80	40	33	73	33
Czech Rep	1997-2012	18.82(2.23)	70	74	57	58	57	29
Denmark	1981-2012	28.18(1.82)	35	23	16	74	18	70
Estonia	1995-2012	25.22(2.73)	82	60	30	60	40	16
Finland	1981-2012	26.47(2.73)	38	59	26	63	33	57
France	1981-2012	24.81(1.11)	63	86	43	71	68	48

Germany	1993-2012	27.23(1.57)	83	65	66	67	35	40
Greece	1981-2012	23.06(4.23)	45	112	57	35	60	50
Hungary	1995-2012	27.40(2.52)	58	82	88	80	46	31
Iceland	1984-2012	17.27(5.52)	28					67
Ireland	1981-2012	29.93(5.44)	24	35	68	70	28	65
Italy	1981-2012	28.37(3.53)	61	75	70	76	50	30
Latvia	1995-2012	22.04(5.60)	69	63	9	70	44	13
Lithuania	2001-2012	18.94(3.12)	82	65	19	60	42	16
Luxembourg	1990-2012	11.80(8.14)	64	70	50	60	40	56
Macedonia	1997-2012	17.20(3.98)	62					35
Malta	1997-2012	20.43(3.19)	47	96	47	59	56	66
Moldova	1996-2012	14.74(3.48)	71					19
Montenegro	2004-2012	-4.68(11.95)	75					20
Morocco	1981-2012	29.35(4.07)	14	68	53	46	70	25
Netherlands	1982-2012	34.27(2.72)	67	53	14	80	38	68
Norway	1981-2006	25.86(3.62)	35	50	8	69	31	55
Poland	1992-2012	22.22(2.18)	38	93	64	60	68	29
Portugal	1981-2012	24.63(4.49)	28	104	31	27	63	33
Romania	1999-2012	19.75(3.58)	52	90	42	30	90	20
Russia	1996-2012	31.42(3.66)	81	95	36	39	93	20
Serbia	2002-2012	12.09(2.87)	52	92	43	25	86	28
Slovak Rep	1995-2008	28.50(2.85)	77	51	110	52	104	28
Slovenia	1994-2012	27.86(1.70)	49	88	19	27	71	48
Spain	1996-2012	24.96(2.58)	48	86	42	51	57	44
Sweden	1981-2012	32.93(2.21)	53	29	5	71	31	78
Switzerland	1990-2012	34.52(2.44)	74	58	70	68	34	66
Ukraine	1997-2012	26.11(5.44)	86					14
United Kingdom	1981-2012	20.04(2.26)	51	35	66	89	35	69
North America		***21.65 (6.00)***	***26.09 (8.91)***	***46.93 (1.01)***	***57 (5.00)***	***85.50 (5.50)***	***39.50 (0.50)***	***63.33 (6.60)***
Canada	1981-2008	26.54(2.23)	36	48	52	80	39	68
Dominican Rep	1991-2012	12.90(3.60)	13					54
United States	1981-2012	23.11(1.96)	26	46	62	91	40	68
South America		***18.78 (5.57)***	***23.45 (8.16)***	***85.32 (7.15)***	***51 (14.55)***	***25.89 (11.46)***	***66.78 (9.32)***	***73 (18.65)***
Argentina	1992-2012	22.23(4.15)	20	86	56	46	49	62
Brazil	1996-2012	22.36(2.58)	44	76	49	38	69	59
Chile	1981-2012	19.47(6.86)	31	86	28	23	63	68
Colombia	1981-2012	15.37(3.16)	13	80	64	13	67	83
El Salvador	1981-2012	13.04(2.58)	20	94	40	19	66	89
Mexico	1981-2012	25.11(4.49)	24	82	69	30	81	97

Peru	1993-2012	18.41(2.66)	25	87	42	16	64	46
Uruguay	1994-2012	16.09(3.11)	26	100	38	36	61	53
Venezuela	1986-2012	19.57(4.14)	16	76	73	12	81	100
Pacific Region		22.87 (4.97)	27 (6.00)	50 (1.00)	59.5 (1.50)	84.5 (5.50)	30 (8.00)	73 (2.00)
Australia	1981-2012	26.50(2.77)	21	51	61	90	38	71
New Zealand	1981-2010	19.01(3.62)	33	49	58	79	22	75

Note: 1. A country (or economy) with the presence of Confucian Temples is defined as a country in Confucian territory. In our sample, Confucian territory includes China, Hong Kong, Indonesia, Japan, South Korea, Malaysia, Singapore, Thailand and Vietnam. The countries in Confucian territory are the same as those in East Asia except the Philippines.
2. The numbers with bold text are regional averages and their standard deviations, which are in parentheses below.

Figure 1 presents the time trends of private saving rates for nine countries classified within the Confucian territory over the 1981–2012 period. Figure 2 illustrates the cross-country distribution of average private saving rates. Figures 3, 4, and 5 depict the distributions of LTO, UA, and IVR scores, respectively. Finally, Figure 6 shows the evolution of average private saving rates across the regions of East Asia, Other Asia, Africa, Europe, North America, and Latin America.

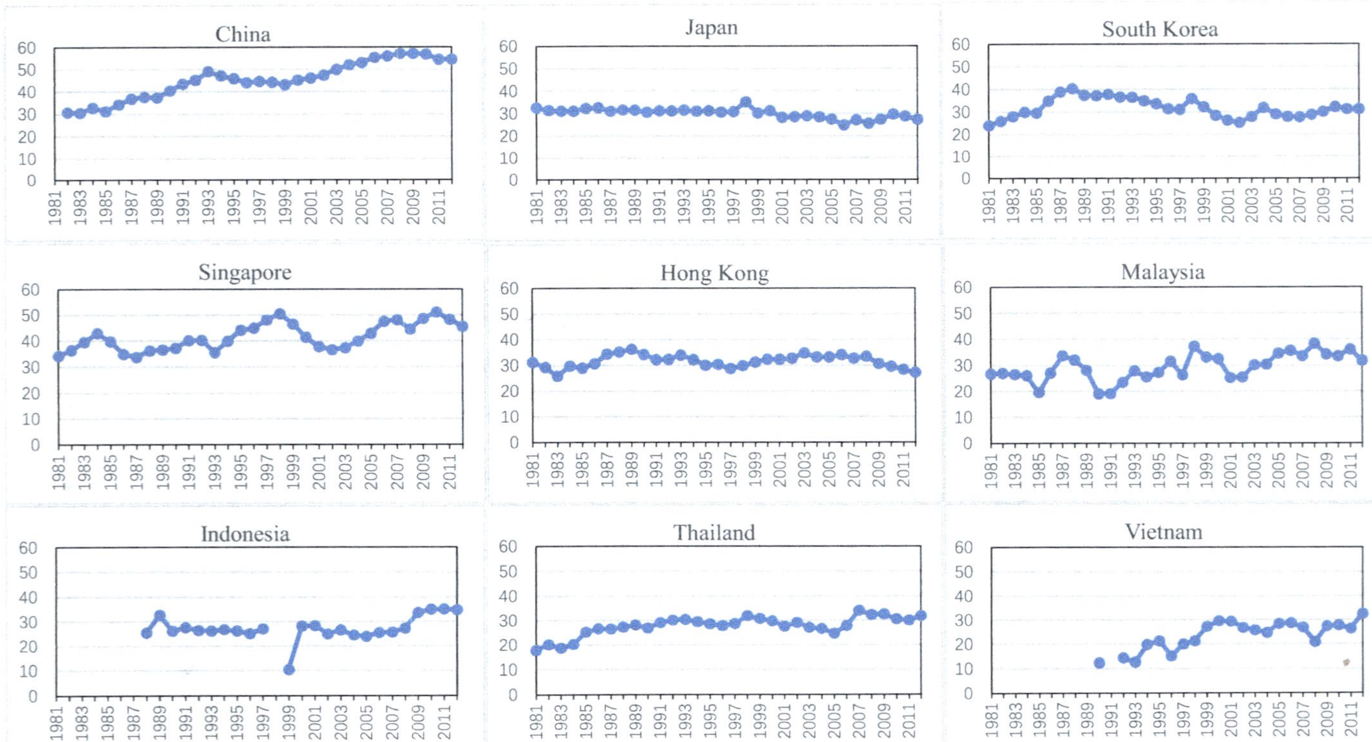

Figure 1: The trends of private saving rates for nine countries in the Confucian territory during our sample period 1981-2012 (the unit in y-axis is %)

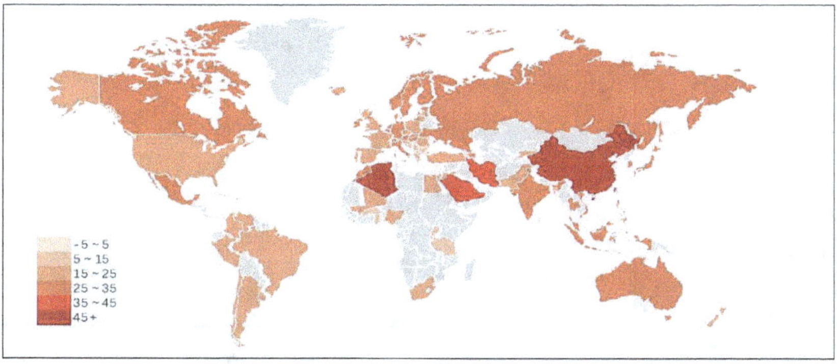

Figure 2 The distribution of average private saving rates around the world

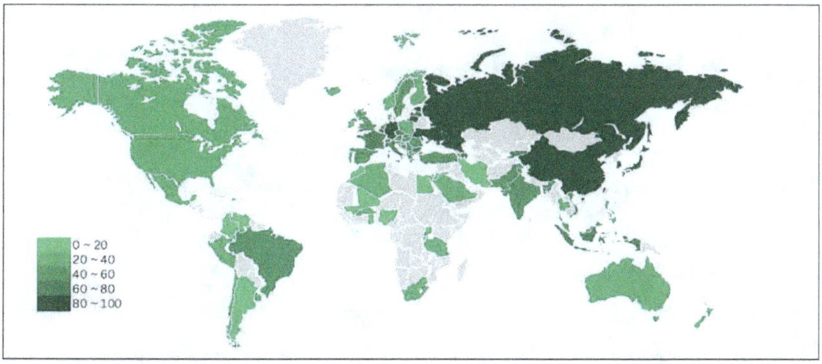

Figure 3 The distribution of long-term orientation (LTO) around the world

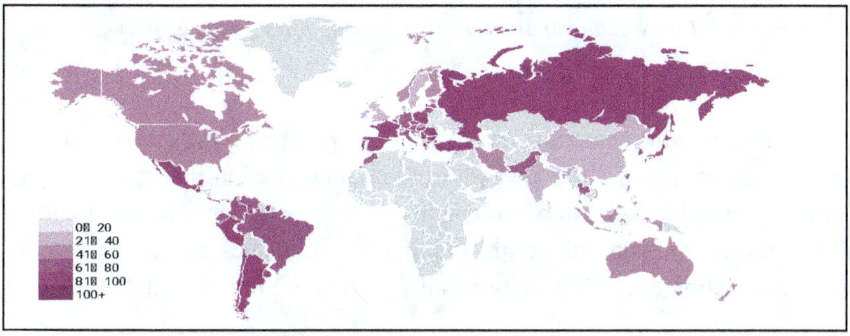

Figure 4 The distribution of uncertainty avoidance (UA) around the world

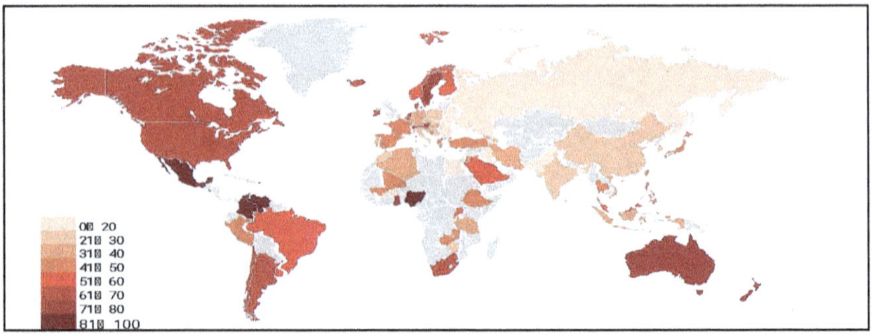

Figure 5 The distribution of indulgence versus restraint (IVR) around the world

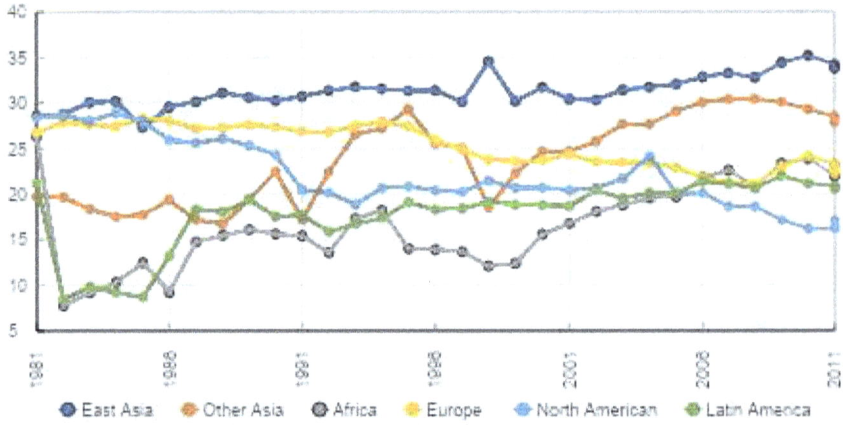

Figure 6 The evolution of average private saving rates for the country-groups

Table 2 reports the summary statistics for the private saving rate, the six Hofstede cultural dimensions, and all related control variables used in this study. Specifically, the table presents the total number of country-year observations, along with the means, standard deviations, and minimum and maximum values for each variable. The pairwise correlation coefficients among all variables are reported in Table 3.

Table 2 Summary statistics for the variables used in this study

This table reports the number of country-year observations (N), mean, standard deviation, minimum and maximum for the variables used in this paper.

Variables	N	Mean	Std.Dev.	Min	Max
Private Saving Rate	1917	23.853	9.830	-25.309	58.936
Long-Term versus Short-Term (*LTO*)	1917	44.372	23.171	4	100
Dummy Variable of Confucian Territory	1917	0.126	0.332	0	1
Ethnic Chinese Population	1471	384.606	1416.55	0.280	9400
Ln (Geographic Distance)	1894	8.915	0.543	6.862	9.868
Genetic Distance	1779	4.126	1.450	0	6.725
Linguistic Distance	1611	0.447	0.311	-1.432	0.526
Uncertainty Avoidance (*UA*)	1445	65.716	24.233	8	112
Hierarchical Religions	1010	47.035	35.315	0	99.300
Real Per Capita GPDI	1917	890.851	105.707	607.614	1051.120
Real Growth Rate of Per Capita GPDI	1917	3.122	7.126	-37.172	87.255
Ln (Terms of Trade)	1917	462.608	21.576	380.102	645.744
Real Deposit Rate	1917	1.094	5.041	-26.010	42.653
Flow of Private Sector Credit/GPDI	1917	7.903	11.215	-125.675	172.971
Inflation	1917	6.121	6.123	-9.320	32.937
Old Age Dependency Ratio	1917	14.984	7.438	3.976	39.043
Share of Urban Population	1917	64.432	21.503	4.855	100
Life Expectancy	1901	71.803	8.526	26.172	83.481
Sovereign Debt Crisis	1917	0.016	0.124	0	1

Table 3 The Correlation coefficients of all variables

Variables	(1)	(2)	(3)	(4)	(5)	(6)	(7)	(8)	(9)	(10)	(11)	(12)	(13)	(14)	(15)	(16)
(1) *Private Saving Rate*	1.00															
(2) *LTO*	0.29	1.00														
(3) *Dummy Variable of Confucian Territory*	0.36	0.38	1.00													
(4) *Ethnic Chinese Population*	0.28	0.15	0.57	1.00												
(5) *Ln (Geographic Distance)*	-0.33	-0.55	-0.67	-0.33	1.00											
(6) *UA*	-0.40	-0.02	-0.31	-0.44	0.26	1.00										
(7) *Real Per Capita GPDI*	0.38	0.32	0.00	0.16	-0.04	-0.02	1.00									
(8) *Real Growth Rate of Per Capita GPDI*	0.11	0.05	0.09	0.01	-0.06	-0.08	-0.13	1.00								
(9) *Ln (Terms of Trade)*	0.06	-0.08	-0.02	-0.02	0.10	0.02	-0.08	0.21	1.00							
(10) *Real Deposit Rate*	-0.08	0.03	0.04	-0.02	0.01	-0.03	0.01	-0.01	-0.07	1.00						
(11) *Flow of Private Sector Credit/GPDI*	0.05	0.07	0.13	0.06	-0.07	-0.16	0.21	0.01	0.01	0.03	1.00					
(12) *Inflation*	-0.17	-0.27	-0.16	-0.14	0.18	0.24	-0.31	0.00	0.03	-0.44	-0.04	1.00				
(13) *Old Age Dependency Ratio*	0.12	0.47	-0.18	-0.14	-0.01	0.15	0.73	-0.11	-0.11	-0.01	0.08	-0.30	1.00			
(14) *Share of Urban Population*	0.30	0.20	0.00	0.25	0.07	-0.01	0.81	-0.10	-0.05	0.07	0.15	-0.17	0.48	1.00		
(15) *Life Expectancy*	0.40	0.36	0.11	0.15	-0.15	-0.04	0.87	-0.08	-0.09	0.10	0.18	-0.33	0.65	0.75	1.00	
(16) *Sovereign Debt Crisis*	-0.04	-0.08	-0.02	-0.03	0.06	0.06	-0.07	-0.03	-0.02	0.01	-0.04	0.15	-0.07	-0.01	-0.06	1.00

5.2 Comparative Analysis Across Country Groups

Several noteworthy findings emerge from the descriptive statistics and graphical analysis. The univariate comparison of private saving rates, Long-Term Orientation (LTO), and Uncertainty Avoidance (UA) across country groups reveals substantial cross-country and cross-regional variation in average private saving behavior.

As reported in Table 1, the highest average private saving rate is observed in Confucian territories (33.08% of GPDI), followed closely by the broader East Asian region (31.62%). The "other Asia" region ranks second overall, with an average private saving rate of 26.27%. In contrast, Africa and Latin America exhibit the lowest average saving rates, at 16.98% and 18.78%, respectively. These figures indicate pronounced regional heterogeneity in private saving behavior.

The results of univariate difference-in-means tests comparing Confucian territories (or East Asia) with other regions are presented in Table 4. For differences A–D, all estimated differences in average private saving rates are positive and statistically significant. This finding suggests that Confucian territories (and, more broadly, East Asia) exhibit significantly higher private saving rates than other regions. Additional (unreported) tests further indicate that "other Asia" ranks second highest in average saving rates, while Africa and Latin America rank lowest and second lowest, respectively.

Table 4 Univariate comparison analysis of private saving rates, LTOs and UAs between Confucian Territory (or East Asia) and other country groups

Countries in group of	Averages of private saving rates (A)	Averages of LTO (B)	Averages of UA (C)	Countries in group of	Averages of private saving rates (D)	Averages of LTO (E)	Averages of UA (F)	Difference (A-D)	Difference (B-E)	Difference (C-F)
Confucian Territory	33.077 (7.927)	67.510 (22.158)	48.983 (28.095)	Other Asia	26.274 (11.687)	40.904 (16.367)	66.196 (13.419)	6.803*** (7.230)	26.607*** (14.015)	-17.213*** (-6.162)
				Africa	16.983 (12.961)	20.331 (10.140)		16.095*** (16.535)	47.180*** (30.567)	
				Europe	24.419 (7.711)	54.946 (18.599)	69.186 (24.050)	8.658*** (15.258)	12.564*** (8.834)	-20.203*** (-10.805)
				North America	21.647 (5.999)	26.086 (8.908)	46.933 (1.006)	11.430*** (11.879)	41.424*** (16.373)	2.050 (0.564)
				South America	18.782 (5.569)	23.445 (8.163)	85.321 (7.145)	14.296*** (22.138)	44.065*** (27.709)	-36.338*** (-18.560)
				Pacific region	22.873 (4.971)	26.806 (6.046)	50.032 (1.008)	10.205*** (9.652)	40.704*** (14.312)	-1.048 (-0.294)
				All Other Countries	22.526 (9.355)	41.045 (21.347)	69.065 (21.911)	10.551*** (16.668)	26.466*** (17.909)	- 20.081*** (-12.342)
East Asia	31.616 (8.548)	62.762 (24.569)	48.399 (26.440)	Other Asia	26.274 (11.687)	40.904 (16.367)	66.196 (13.419)	5.342*** (5.724)	21.858*** (10.866)	-17.797*** (-6.771)
				Africa	16.983 (12.961)	20.331 (10.140)		14.634*** (15.371)	42.431*** (25.441)	
				Europe	24.419 (7.711)	54.946 (18.599)	69.186 (24.050)	7.197*** (13.025)	7.816*** (5.541)	-20.787*** (-11.826)
				North America	21.647 (5.999)	26.086 (8.908)	46.933 (1.006)	9.969*** (9.800)	36.675*** (13.169)	1.466 (0.429)

				South America	18.782 (5.569)	23.445 (8.163)	85.321 (7.145)	12.834*** (19.156)	39.317*** (22.646)	-36.922*** (-20.039)
				Pacific region	22.873 (4.971)	26.806 (6.046)	50.032 (1.008)	8.743*** (7.756)	35.955*** (11.432)	-1.633 (-0.486)
				All Other Countries	22.564 (9.429)	41.318 (21.463)	69.749 (21.808)	9.052*** (14.880)	21.444*** (14.961)	-21.350*** (-13.963)

Note: On the last three columns, t-statistics are in parentheses. For other columns, standard errors are in parentheses. Significance at the 10%, 5%, and 1% level is indicated by *, **, ***, respectively.

With regard to cultural dimensions, similar difference-in-means tests (differences B–E and C–F) show that Confucian territories (or East Asia) exhibit significantly higher average LTO scores and lower average UA scores relative to most other regions. The main exceptions are North America and the Pacific region. In particular, the t-statistics indicate no statistically significant differences in average UA between Confucian territories (or East Asia), North America, and the Pacific region.

Further comparative analysis reveals that the average IVR score is lowest among "other Asian countries" and highest in South America, although the detailed results are not tabulated. These patterns are broadly consistent with the theoretical predictions that more restrained cultures (low IVR) tend to exhibit stronger saving behavior, whereas more indulgent cultures (high IVR) are associated with lower saving rates.

Finally, a similar comparative analysis shows that both Africa and South America exhibit lower LTO and higher IVR, which seems to explain why their saving rates are the lowest.

The above inference is a preliminary estimation based on the results in Table 4. The formal statistical tests will be presented in the following subsections.

5.3 Baseline Regression Results (Tests of Hypotheses 1, 2 and 4)

The regression results for Equation (1) are presented in Table 5. In these estimations, private saving rates are regressed on the six cultural dimensions proposed by Geert Hofstede—Long-Term Orientation (LTO), Uncertainty Avoidance (UA), Masculinity (MAS), Individualism (IND), Power Distance (PD), and Indulgence versus Restraint (IVR)—along with the set of macroeconomic control variables. The sample covers the full period from 1981 to 2012.

Table 5 The result of baseline regression (Equation (1))

This table reports the result of baseline regression as the following equation

$$Private\_Saving\_Rate_{it} = \alpha + \beta CulturalProxy_i + \gamma Control_{it} + \varphi_t + \varepsilon_{it}$$

The scores of six cultural dimensions in Hofstede et al. (2010) are used as cultural proxies. The dependent variable is private saving rates. All parameters are estimated by using pooled ordinary least squares (OLS) with standard errors adjusted for clustering by country. Cultural proxies include scores of *LTO* on 84 countries, scores of *UA*, *MAS*, *IND* and *PD* on 61 countries, scores of *IVR* on 82 countries. The sample periods of private saving rates for each country are listed in Table 1. Robust standard errors clustered at the country level are in parentheses. Significance at the 10%, 5%, and 1% level is indicated by *, **, ***, respectively.

Variables	**(1)**	**(2)**	**(3)**	**(4)**	**(5)**	**(6)**	**(7)**	**(8)**
LTO		0.126***						0.128***
		(0.040)						(0.035)
UA			-0.109***					-0.110***
			(0.037)					(0.030)
MAS				-0.010				
				(0.037)				
IND					0.009			
					(0.045)			
PD						0.019		
						(0.037)		
IVR							-0.103**	
							(0.040)	
Ln (Real Per Capita GPDI)	0.068***	0.070***	0.049***	0.052***	0.051***	0.053***	0.076***	0.056***
	(0.013)	(0.012)	(0.017)	(0.018)	(0.017)	(0.017)	(0.014)	(0.014)
Real Growth Rate of Per Capita GPDI	0.213***	0.166***	0.330***	0.354***	0.358***	0.355***	0.180***	0.260***
	(0.074)	(0.057)	(0.071)	(0.088)	(0.082)	(0.082)	(0.067)	(0.056)
Ln (Terms of Trade)	0.021	0.029	0.004	-0.003	-0.004	-0.004	0.026	0.013
	(0.032)	(0.028)	(0.024)	(0.027)	(0.026)	(0.027)	(0.029)	(0.020)
Real Deposit Rate	-0.312***	-0.283***	-0.127	-0.216*	-0.217*	-0.216*	-0.275***	-0.039
	(0.111)	(0.106)	(0.113)	(0.130)	(0.128)	(0.128)	(0.102)	(0.109)
Flow of Private Sector Credit/GPDI	-0.039	-0.051	-0.058	-0.021	-0.020	-0.017	-0.040	-0.072*
	(0.053)	(0.044)	(0.044)	(0.061)	(0.058)	(0.058)	(0.051)	(0.038)
Inflation	-0.249**	-0.163	-0.088	-0.281**	-0.277*	-0.288**	-0.201*	0.051
	(0.120)	(0.105)	(0.141)	(0.137)	(0.147)	(0.141)	(0.110)	(0.128)
Old Age Dependency Ratio	-0.499***	-0.686***	-0.261*	-0.390**	-0.395**	-0.363*	-0.604***	-0.413***
	(0.151)	(0.147)	(0.153)	(0.186)	(0.180)	(0.182)	(0.158)	(0.124)
Share of Urban	-0.044	-0.046	-0.098**	-0.096**	-0.094*	-0.092*	-0.016	-0.107**

Population	(0.046)	(0.044)	(0.047)	(0.046)	(0.048)	(0.047)	(0.046)	(0.043)
Intercept	-31.420*	-41.051***	-1.503	-3.694	-3.217	-5.782	-36.392**	-15.949
	(16.907)	(14.766)	(17.821)	(19.068)	(18.321)	(18.576)	(15.772)	(14.074)
N	1917	1917	1445	1445	1445	1445	1842	1445
Year dummy	yes	yes	yes	yes	yes	yes	yes	yes
Adj. R^2	0.247	0.314	0.270	0.176	0.176	0.177	0.289	0.379

The results indicate that three cultural dimensions—LTO, UA, and IVR—have statistically significant effects on private saving rates across countries.[22]

First, the coefficient on LTO is positive and statistically significant at the 1% level, indicating that countries with stronger long-term orientation exhibit higher private saving rates. This finding provides strong support for Hypothesis 1 and is consistent with the view that long-term oriented cultures emphasize thrift, perseverance, and future-oriented planning.

Second, the coefficient on UA is negative and statistically significant at the 1% level. This suggests that higher uncertainty avoidance is associated with lower private saving rates, thereby supporting Hypothesis 2. In other words, individuals in low-UA societies appear more likely to maintain or even increase saving when facing uncertainty, whereas those in high-UA societies tend to reduce saving under similar conditions.

Third, the coefficient on IVR is negative and statistically significant at the 5% level. Although the level of statistical significance is weaker than for LTO and UA, the result nonetheless supports Hypothesis 4, implying that more indulgent societies (high IVR) tend to exhibit lower private saving rates, while more restrained societies (low IVR) display stronger saving behavior.

With respect to the control variables, the estimated coefficients are broadly consistent with those reported by Grigoli et al (2018). Real per capita GPDI and the real growth rate of per capita GPDI both exert positive and statistically significant effects on private saving rates. In contrast, the real deposit interest rate and the old-age dependency ratio are found to have statistically significant negative effects. These findings are consistent with standard consumption theory and demographic life-cycle

[22] In order to check the robustness of our finding that LTO and UA both have significant impacts on private saving rates around the world, we split the full sample period into two sub-sample periods: 1981-2000 and 2001-2012. Then we re-estimate the baseline regression using the five cultural indices (without IVR) obtained from Hofstede and Hofstede (2005) for the first sub-sample period; these five cultural indices are based upon their 1985 and 1997 surveys. We, however, reduce the number of sample countries from 84 in the full-sample period to 32 for LTO, and from 61 to 54 for IND, UA, PD and MAS based upon the lack of availability of data. Similarly, we re-estimate the baseline regression using the six cultural dimensions obtained from Hofstede et al. (2010) for the second sub-sample period and employ the same number of countries as the full-sample period used in Table 5. The estimated results, which are reported in Appendix Table A1 and A2, show that the coefficients of LTO and UA are all significant for both regressions, implying that they remain consistent with those reported in Table 5.

considerations.

Model (1) in Table 5 excludes the cultural proxies and therefore serves as the benchmark specification. This baseline model explains approximately 24.7% of the variation in private saving rates ($R^2 = 0.247$).

Comparisons between Model (1) and Models (2), (3), (7), and (8) demonstrate that the inclusion of cultural proxies substantially improves explanatory power. Specifically:

- The inclusion of LTO increases the R^2 from 24.7% to 31.4% (an increase of 6.7 percentage points).
- The inclusion of UA increases the R^2 to 27.0% (an increase of 2.3 percentage points).
- The inclusion of IVR increases the R^2 to 28.9% (an increase of 4.2 percentage points).
- When multiple cultural proxies, LTO and UA, are included jointly, the R^2 rises to 37.9%, representing a 13.2 percentage-point increase relative to the benchmark model.[23]

These increases in explanatory power indicate that cultural dimensions play a non-trivial role in explaining cross-country variations in private saving rates.

Importantly, the coefficients on the macroeconomic control variables in Model (1) remain stable and statistically significant after the inclusion of the cultural proxies in subsequent models. This stability suggests that the cultural variables are not simply proxying for the included macroeconomic fundamentals and are reasonably orthogonal to the baseline controls. Hence, the addition of cultural dimensions meaningfully enhances the model's ability to account for variation in private saving behavior across countries.

5.4 Interaction Model and Conditional Impact of the Cultural Proxies (Tests of Hypothesis 2)

In the baseline regressions reported in Models (1)-(8) of Table 5, the estimated coefficients on the income-related control variable, $ln(Real\ Per\ Capita\ GPDI)$, are consistently positive and statistically significant at the 1% level. This result indicates

[23] In Section 1, several other factors that affect the private savings rate were mentioned. Although they also have explanatory power, it is far smaller than the additional 13.2% explanatory power attributed to cultural factors here. Therefore, we can conclude that cultural factors play a dominant role in shaping private saving rates globally.

that higher income levels are associated with higher private saving rates, implying a positive marginal effect of income on saving behavior.

However, the baseline specifications estimate only the unconditional marginal effect of income on private saving rates. It is plausible that, for a given country, this marginal effect depends on its national cultural characteristics. In other words, cultural attributes may moderate the sensitivity of private saving to income changes.

To examine this possibility, we estimate the following interaction model:

$$Private\_Saving\_Rate_{it} = \alpha + \beta CulturalProxy_i + \theta CulturalProxy_i * Ln\,(Real\ Per\ Capita\ GPDI)_{it} + \lambda Ln\,(Real\ Per\ Capita\ GPDI)_{it} + \gamma Control_{it} + \varphi_t + \varepsilon_{it}. \quad (2)$$

In this specification, the interaction term between the cultural proxy and income allows the marginal effect of income on private saving to vary across cultural contexts.

Based on Equation (2), the marginal effect of income on private saving rates, conditional on national cultural attributes, is given by:

$$\frac{\partial E(Private\_Saving\_Rate_{it})}{\partial Ln\,(Real\ Per\ Capita\ GPDI)_{it}} = \hat{\lambda} + \hat{\theta} CulturalProxy_i \quad (3)$$

Equation (3) shows that the conditional marginal effect depends on the estimated interaction coefficient $\hat{\theta}$. If $\hat{\theta} = 0$, national cultural attributes have no moderating (conditional) impact on the income–saving relationship. A statistically significant $\hat{\theta}$ would indicate that the responsiveness of private saving rates to income varies systematically with cultural characteristics.

The estimation results of the interaction models are reported in Table 6, where the estimated coefficients on the interaction term $\hat{\theta}$ are highlighted in bold. The interaction models employ the same set of control variables and fixed effects as those used in the baseline regressions presented in Table 5.

Table 6 The result of interaction regression (Equation (2))

This table reports the result of interaction regression as the following equation

$$Private\_Saving\_Rate_{it} = \alpha + \beta CulturalProxy_i + \theta CulturalProxy_i * Ln\ (Real\ Per\ Capita\ GPDI)_{it} + \lambda Ln\ (Real\ Per\ Capita\ GPDI)_{it} + \gamma Control_{it} + \varphi_t + \varepsilon_{it}$$

The scores of six cultural dimensions in Hofstede et al. (2010) are used as cultural proxies. The dependent variable is private saving rates. All parameters are estimated by using pooled ordinary least squares (OLS) with standard errors adjusted for clustering by country. Cultural proxies include scores of LTO on 84 countries, scores of UA, MAS, IND and PD on 61 countries, scores of IVR on 82 countries. The sample periods of private saving rates for each country are listed in Table 1. The conditional impact of national cultural attribute on the marginal effect of individual income level on the private saving rates is determined by the estimated coefficient of $\hat{\theta}$ (bold text). Robust standard errors clustered at the country level are in parentheses. Significance at the 10%, 5%, and 1% level is indicated by *, **, ***, respectively.

Variables	**(1)**	**(2)**	**(3)**	**(4)**	**(5)**	**(6)**
	LTO	*UA*	*MAS*	*IND*	*PD*	*IVR*
LTO	0.490					
	(0.328)					
UA		-1.308**				
		(0.556)				
MAS			1.154			
			(0.804)			
IND				0.618		
				(0.482)		
PD					0.394	
					(0.515)	
IVR						-0.323
						(0.400)
CulturalProxy * Ln (Real Per Capita GPDI)	**-0.410×10^{-3}**	**0.127×10^{-2}****	**-0.122×10^{-2}**	**-0.632×10^{-3}**	**-0.395×10^{-3}**	**0.250×10^{-3}**
	(0.346×10^{-3})	**(0.583×10^{-3})**	**(0.829×10^{-3})**	**(0.495×10^{-3})**	**(0.535×10^{-3})**	**(0.439×10^{-3})**

Ln (Real Per Capita GPDI)	0.084***	-0.021	0.117***	0.074**	0.079**	0.064**
	(0.018)	(0.041)	(0.038)	(0.028)	(0.035)	(0.025)
Real Growth Rate of Per Capita GPDI	0.152***	0.316***	0.370***	0.346***	0.367***	0.185***
	(0.050)	(0.065)	(0.086)	(0.087)	(0.085)	(0.067)
Ln (Terms of Trade)	0.033	-0.002	-0.005	-0.001	-0.007	0.026
	(0.026)	(0.021)	(0.027)	(0.026)	(0.026)	(0.029)
Real Deposit Rate	-0.330***	-0.117	-0.219*	-0.205	-0.215*	-0.276***
	(0.118)	(0.095)	(0.127)	(0.127)	(0.127)	(0.103)
Flow of Private Sector Credit/GPDI	-0.059	-0.079**	-0.024	-0.015	-0.020	-0.041
	(0.038)	(0.036)	(0.054)	(0.057)	(0.055)	(0.050)
Inflation	-0.199*	0.002	-0.278**	-0.292**	-0.268*	-0.182*
	(0.108)	(0.133)	(0.138)	(0.140)	(0.140)	(0.105)
Old Age Dependency Ratio	-0.681***	-0.336**	-0.383**	-0.424**	-0.356*	-0.607***
	(0.146)	(0.145)	(0.183)	(0.179)	(0.187)	(0.155)
Share of Urban Population	-0.040	-0.061	-0.102**	-0.109**	-0.083*	-0.012
	(0.043)	(0.045)	(0.046)	(0.047)	(0.048)	(0.046)
Intercept	-55.382***	64.880*	-64.332*	-24.933	-30.637	-27.068
	(17.176)	(37.029)	(38.096)	(28.762)	(37.850)	(23.660)
N	1917	1445	1445	1445	1445	1842
Year dummy	yes	yes	yes	yes	yes	yes
Adj. R^2	0.322	0.328	0.206	0.188	0.181	0.291

Through this specification, we directly test whether cultural dimensions—particularly Uncertainty Avoidance (UA), as suggested in Hypothesis 2—moderate the marginal propensity to save out of income. A significant interaction effect would imply that the strength of the income–saving relationship differs across cultural environments, thereby providing additional insight into how national culture shapes private saving behavior beyond its direct (unconditional) effect.

The results reported in bold in Table 6 indicate that only Uncertainty Avoidance (UA) exhibits a statistically significant conditional effect (at the 5% level) on the marginal impact of real per capita GPDI on private saving rates. The estimated interaction coefficient is positive, implying that UA moderates the income–saving relationship.

Specifically, the positive interaction term suggests that the marginal effect of income on private saving becomes stronger as UA increases. In practical terms, private saving rates in low-UA countries (such as those in East Asia) are relatively less sensitive to changes in income levels, whereas private saving rates in high-UA countries (such as those in Latin America) respond more strongly to income fluctuations.

This finding is consistent with Hypothesis 2, which posits that individuals in low uncertainty avoidance societies are more comfortable with uncertain or ambiguous situations and therefore tend to maintain their normal saving levels even during periods of economic instability or financial crisis. By contrast, individuals in high-UA countries are more likely to adjust their saving behavior in response to income changes.

The results therefore provide an additional explanation for the persistence of high private saving rates in low-UA economies, particularly those in East Asia: cultural tolerance toward uncertainty reduces the sensitivity of saving behavior to short-term income fluctuations, reinforcing long-run saving stability.

5.5 Confucianism as the Common Cultural Core of East Asian Countries (Test of Hypothesis 3)

The baseline regression results indicate that high LTO and low UA help to explain the elevated private saving rates observed in East Asian countries. As discussed earlier, Confucianism may be regarded as the shared cultural foundation of these societies. We therefore proceed to test Hypothesis 3, which predicts that countries characterized by Confucian norms will exhibit higher private saving rates.

To operationalize Confucianism empirically, we adopt three alternative proxy variables.

First, consistent with prior literature, Confucian norms are proxied by the historical presence of Confucian temples. The first proxy is therefore a *Dummy Variable of Confucian Territory*, which takes the value of 1 if a country (or economy) historically maintains Confucian temples, and 0 otherwise.[24] This measure captures the institutional and historical embeddedness of Confucian traditions.

Second, following Rauch and Trindade (2002) and Huang, Jin and Qian (2013), we use the *Ethnic Chinese population share* as an alternative proxy. This variable is defined as the proportion of ethnic Chinese individuals in a country's total population. Since Confucian values strongly influence overseas Chinese communities, this measure captures the diffusion of Confucian norms beyond mainland China.[25]

Third, following the cultural-distance approach of Aggarwal, Kearney and Lucey (2012), we employ *Geographical Distance* as a proxy for cultural proximity to the Confucian core. Specifically, we measure the Great Circle Distance (GCD) between Beijing and the official capital (or the most populous city) of each country. Greater geographical distance is interpreted as reflecting weaker exposure to Confucian cultural influence.

The regression results for these three proxy variables are presented in columns (1)–(3) of Table 7. The findings indicate that the coefficients on the Dummy Variable of Confucian Territory and Geographical Distance are statistically significant at the 1% level, while the coefficient on Ethnic Chinese population share is significant at the 10% level. Importantly, all estimated signs are consistent with theoretical predictions:

- The Dummy Variable of Confucian Territory has a positive and significant effect on private saving rates.
- The Ethnic Chinese population share also exhibits a positive association with private saving.
- Geographical Distance shows a negative and significant effect, indicating that countries located farther from Beijing—and thus presumably less influenced by Confucian norms—tend to have lower private saving rates.

---

[24] See Kung and Ma (2014), Du (2015, 2016) and Chen, Jin, Ma and Xu (2019) in which it is noted that the inheritance of Confucian virtues can be achieved through the construction of Confucian Temples, where the beliefs and values of Confucianism are better disseminated among local society and transmitted from one generation to another.

[25] The importance of overseas Chinese networks in overcoming informal barriers in China was examined by Rauch and Trindade (2002) on international trade, and by Huang et al. (2013) on FDI inflows. Both studies found that the ethnic and cultural ties in Chinese networks, proxied by ethnic Chinese population shares, led to increased bilateral trade and FDI inflows. The data on ethnic Chinese population shares are provided in Poston and Wong (2016).

Table 7 The result of three proxies of Confucianism as the common cultural core of East Asian countries

This table reports the estimated result of baseline regression with three proxies of Confucianism as the common cultural core of the East Asian countries. The dependent variable is private saving rates. All parameters are estimated using pooled OLS with standard errors adjusted for clustering by country. In columns (1) to (3), control variables are same as those in baseline regression in Table 5. In columns (4) to (8), additional demographic variable and the dummy variable of sovereign debt crisis period are included as the extra control variables. Robust standard errors clustered at the country level are in parentheses. Significance at the 10%, 5%, and 1% level is indicated by *, **, ***, respectively.

Variables	**(1)**	**(2)**	**(3)**	**(4)**	**(5)**	**(6)**	**(7)**	**(8)**
LTO				0.117^{***}				
				(0.036)				
UA					-0.106^{***}			
					(0.035)			
Dummy Variable of	8.969^{***}					7.764^{***}		
Confucian Territory	(2.581)					(2.416)		
Ethnic Chinese		0.001^{*}					0.001^{*}	
Population Share		(0.001)					(0.001)	
Ln (Geographic			-5.413^{***}					-5.139^{***}
Distance)			(1.298)					(1.404)
Ln (Real Per Capita	0.060^{***}	0.055^{***}	0.064^{***}	0.048^{***}	0.029	0.043^{***}	0.047^{***}	0.058^{***}
GPDI)	(0.013)	(0.014)	(0.012)	(0.015)	(0.022)	(0.016)	(0.017)	(0.014)
Real Growth Rate of Per	0.170^{***}	0.233^{***}	0.123^{***}	0.154^{***}	0.330^{***}	0.163^{***}	0.232^{***}	0.124^{***}
Capita GPDI	(0.058)	(0.052)	(0.046)	(0.051)	(0.067)	(0.054)	(0.051)	(0.045)
Ln (Terms of Trade)	0.030	0.048^{*}	0.041	0.033	0.010	0.033	0.051^{**}	0.042
	(0.031)	(0.025)	(0.029)	(0.029)	(0.024)	(0.031)	(0.025)	(0.029)
Real Deposit Rate	-0.258^{**}	-0.205^{*}	-0.196^{*}	-0.342^{***}	-0.178^{*}	-0.312^{***}	-0.223^{**}	-0.214^{*}
	(0.101)	(0.106)	(0.104)	(0.110)	(0.103)	(0.108)	(0.104)	(0.114)
Flow of Private Sector	-0.073^{**}	-0.077^{***}	-0.101^{***}	-0.056	-0.072^{*}	-0.073^{**}	-0.077^{***}	-0.101^{***}
Credit/GPDI	(0.037)	(0.026)	(0.028)	(0.039)	(0.038)	(0.035)	(0.025)	(0.027)

Inflation	-0.115	-0.195*	-0.070	-0.181*	-0.050	-0.140	-0.185*	-0.084
	(0.109)	(0.106)	(0.105)	(0.101)	(0.134)	(0.106)	(0.106)	(0.106)
Old Age Dependency Ratio	-0.329**	-0.269	-0.455***	-0.701***	-0.302**	-0.375**	-0.282*	-0.465***
	(0.163)	(0.163)	(0.136)	(0.147)	(0.143)	(0.166)	(0.161)	(0.140)
Share of Urban Population	-0.035	-0.104**	0.001	-0.070	-0.118**	-0.055	-0.108**	-0.008
	(0.042)	(0.042)	(0.042)	(0.046)	(0.050)	(0.045)	(0.042)	(0.044)
Life Expectancy				0.403**	0.576	0.320*	0.158	0.114
				(0.181)	(0.347)	(0.179)	(0.157)	(0.169)
Sovereign Debt Crisis				0.990	2.563	0.383	-0.236	0.930
				(2.054)	(2.155)	(2.188)	(2.375)	(1.984)
Intercept	-34.524**	-32.389**	4.777	-48.713***	-25.523	-40.750**	-37.481**	0.576
	(16.481)	(15.101)	(17.542)	(15.574)	(19.127)	(16.632)	(15.387)	(19.320)
N	1917	1471	1894	1901	1445	1901	1471	1878
Year dummy	yes	yes	yes	yes	yes	yes	yes	yes
Adj. R^2	0.326	0.260	0.379	0.341	0.295	0.340	0.264	0.380

Taken together, these results provide empirical support for Hypothesis 3, suggesting that Confucianism, as a deep-rooted cultural tradition, contributes to higher private saving behavior across countries.

In summary, the findings of this section demonstrate that four key cultural variables—Confucianism, Long-Term Orientation (LTO), Uncertainty Avoidance (UA), and Indulgence versus Restraint (IVR)—exert statistically significant effects on private saving rates across countries. These results underscore the importance of cultural factors in explaining cross-country heterogeneity in saving behavior.

Our evidence also provides a potential resolution to the longstanding "East Asian saving puzzle." Specifically, the relatively high LTO scores observed in China, Japan, and other East Asian economies help explain their elevated levels of private saving. The cultural emphasis on perseverance, thrift, and long-term planning fosters a structural propensity toward higher saving. At the same time, the relatively low UA scores in these economies help explain the persistence and stability of their high saving rates, even during periods of macroeconomic instability or financial crisis. Lower uncertainty avoidance appears to reduce the sensitivity of saving behavior to income fluctuations, thereby reinforcing long-run saving stability.

In addition, the comparative analysis in Section 5.2 reveals that "other Asian countries" exhibit the lowest average IVR scores, whereas South America displays the highest. Given the estimated negative relationship between IVR and private saving rates, these patterns suggest that restrained cultures (low IVR) are associated with stronger saving behavior, while indulgent cultures (high IVR) are linked to lower saving rates. Thus, cultural restraint may help explain the relatively high saving rates observed in other Asian economies, while cultural indulgence may account for the comparatively low saving rates in South America.

Finally, cultural indulgence (high IVR) combined with a short-term orientation (low LTO) likewise explains why Africa has the lowest private saving rate.

Taken together, these findings highlight that cultural attributes not only influence saving levels directly but also shape the stability and responsiveness of saving behavior over time, thereby playing a fundamental role in the cross-country distribution of private saving rates.

6. ROBUSTNESS TESTS AND EXTENSIONS

We now go on to carry out robustness checks for potential endogeneity in the instrumental variable regression in order to verify our results, and also present some critical extensions aimed at dealing with the problem of omitted variables.

6.1 Omitted Variables Concerns

In the previous sections, Long-Term Orientation (LTO) and Uncertainty Avoidance (UA) were found to exert significant positive and negative effects, respectively, on private saving rates. However, these results may be subject to potential endogeneity concerns, defined as a situation in which the cultural proxy is correlated with the regression error term. Such endogeneity could lead to biased and inconsistent estimates of the effects of LTO or UA on private saving behavior.

A primary concern relates to omitted variables that may be correlated with both cultural dimensions (LTO or UA) and private saving rates. To address this issue, we augment our baseline specification by including three additional demographic variables in the regressions reported in Table 7:

1. Life expectancy
2. Young-age dependency ratio
3. A dummy variable for the sovereign debt crisis period

Although the inclusion of these variables reduces the sample size due to data availability constraints, it allows for a more stringent test of our hypotheses.[26]

According to the life-cycle hypothesis, individuals tend to dissave when young, save modestly during early adulthood, save substantially during middle age, and dissave again after retirement. Therefore, the theory predicts that life expectancy should have a positive effect on saving rates, while both old-age and young-age dependency ratios should exert negative effects.[27]

As shown in columns (4)–(8) of Table 7, the estimated coefficients on LTO, UA, and the three proxies of Confucianism (the Dummy Variable of Confucian Territory, Ethnic Chinese Population Share, and Geographical Distance) remain statistically significant and maintain their expected signs after controlling for these additional demographic factors. These findings substantially reduce concerns that our main

[26] The data on *Life expectancy* and the *Young-age dependency ratio* were obtained from the World Bank World Development Indicators. Due to data limitations, the Gini coefficients are not included as additional control variables.

[27] As a result of the presence of collinearity diagnostics when including both *Old-* and *Young-age dependency ratios*, the *Young-age dependency ratio* was dropped from the regression specification.

results are driven by omitted demographic variables.

A second potential concern is reverse causality—namely, the possibility that private saving behavior influences national cultural characteristics such as LTO or UA. Conceptually, this concern appears limited. Informal institutions such as culture evolve gradually over long historical periods and are generally regarded as fundamental determinants of formal institutions and economic outcomes. As argued by Oliver Williamson (2000), culture operates at a deeper institutional level and typically precedes formal economic arrangements.

From an empirical perspective, the cultural scores reported in Hofstede et al. (2010) are based on survey data collected prior to our 1981–2012 sample period. This temporal ordering further mitigates concerns regarding reverse causality, as it is unlikely that contemporaneous private saving rates systematically influenced previously measured cultural values.

Finally, measurement error in the cultural variables—particularly LTO and UA—may also pose a concern. Since these indices are constructed from survey-based responses and standardized at the country level, any noise in measurement could attenuate estimated coefficients. In the following subsection, we address these remaining endogeneity concerns using an instrumental variable (IV) approach.

6.2 Instrumental Variable Approach

To further address the endogeneity concerns discussed above, we follow several prior cultural-economics studies and employ an instrumental variable (IV) approach.[28] The IV framework allows us to isolate the variation in the cultural proxy that is plausibly exogenous to private saving behavior, thereby facilitating consistent estimation of the causal effects of culture on saving rates.

The IV methodology relies on additional variables—referred to as instruments—that shift the cultural proxy while remaining uncorrelated with the regression error term. For an instrument to be valid, it must satisfy two key conditions:

1. *Relevance condition*: Conditional on other exogenous controls, the instrument must be sufficiently correlated with the cultural proxy.
2. *Exclusion restriction*: The instrument must affect private saving rates only through its effect on the cultural proxy and must not be directly correlated with the error term.

[28] Examples include Barro and McCleary (2003), Guiso, Sapienza and Zingales (2016), Ahern, Daminelli and Fracassi (2015), along with many other related culture and finance papers.

Under these conditions, the IV estimator can address potential bias arising from omitted variables, reverse causality, or measurement error.[29]

6.2.1 LTO Instruments

Following the argument of Luigi Luca Cavalli-Sforza (2001), genetic, linguistic, and cultural characteristics of societies are often correlated due to historical processes of transmission and migration. Since genes, languages, and cultural values are transmitted intergenerationally, countries that are genetically or linguistically closer are more likely to share similar cultural traits. Accordingly, we employ *Genetic Distance* and *Linguistic Distance* as instruments for Long-Term Orientation (LTO).[30]

(1) Genetic Distance

To quantify genetic heterogeneity across countries, we use the fixation index (Fst distance) developed by Cavalli-Sforza, Menozzi and Piazza (1994).[31] The Fst index measures the degree of genetic differentiation between populations.

In constructing our instrument, we follow the "frontier method" proposed by Spolaore and Wacziarg (2009).[32] Since South Korea exhibits the highest score on the Hofstede LTO index in our sample, we designate South Korea as the cultural "frontier." Genetic Distance is therefore defined as the absolute difference between the Fst value of a given country and that of South Korea. A higher value of this measure indicates greater genetic divergence from the LTO frontier country.

The underlying logic is that countries genetically closer to South Korea are more likely to share long-term oriented cultural traits, while genetic distance captures deep-rooted historical divergence that is plausibly exogenous to contemporary private saving rates.

(2) Linguistic Distance

For linguistic distance,[33] we adopt the composite index developed by Dow and

---

[29] We do not address the endogeneity issue of IVR, as its statistical significance is only 5%.

[30] Whilst Nash and Patel (2019) comprehensively described and evaluated the instruments used in the prior culture and finance literature, they compiled a total of 19 potential instruments for only eight national cultural value dimensions – Individualism, Uncertainty Avoidance, Power Distance, Masculinity (Hofstede, 1980), Egalitarianism, Harmony, Embeddedness (Siegel, Licht and Schwartz, 2013) and Trust (Aghion, Algan, Cahuc and Shleifer 2010) – with no potential instruments being reviewed for the LTO cultural dimension. They explained that LTO was not widely adopted at that time within the culture and finance literature; thus, to the best of our knowledge, our study is the first to adopt Genetic distance and Linguistic distance as LTO instruments.

[31] Examples include Ahern, Daminelli and Fracassi (2015), Bryan, Nash and Patel (2015), Eun, Wang and Xiao (2015) and Gorodnichenko and Roland (2017). We also employ the genetic distance matched to populations as they were in 1500 AD, as described in Spolaore and Wacziarg (2018), in order to avoid any potential endogeneity.

[32] A 'frontier' refers to a country which has an outlier value in a specific cultural dimension. Based upon studies in the US of the effects of individualism (Eun et al., 2015) and in Singapore on the effects of uncertainty avoidance (Bryan et al., 2015), both served as frontier countries, because the US (Singapore) scored the highest (lowest) on Hofstede's Individualism and Uncertainty Avoidance indices.

[33] The Linguistic distance data were obtained from Dow and Karunaratna (2006).

Karunaratna. Their measure consists of three components:

- *L1*: A five-point Likert-type scale capturing structural differences between the major languages of two countries.
- *L2* and *L3*: Two additional five-point scales measuring the incidence and diffusion of one country's major language within another country.

These three components are combined using factor analysis to generate a single composite index of Linguistic Distance. Higher values indicate greater linguistic differences between countries.

As with genetic distance, linguistic distance captures historical and structural divergence that shapes cultural traits over long horizons but is unlikely to be directly influenced by contemporary saving behavior. Hence, it plausibly satisfies the exclusion restriction, conditional on the included controls.

This IV strategy allows us to exploit deep historical determinants of culture to identify the exogenous component of LTO. In the next subsection, we report the first-stage and second-stage estimation results and assess the strength and validity of these instruments.

6.2.2 UA Instruments

Hofstede (1983) argued that those countries with high UA scores will tend to establish societies emphasizing order and predictability, and gravitate towards religions that are more rigidly structured and more likely to claim 'absolute truth'. Hofstede et al. (2010) further emphasized that by claiming knowledge of life after death, religion helps people to cope with an unpredictable future by giving them an ultimate certainty. La Porta, Lopez-de-Silanes, Shleifer and Vishny (1997) noted that hierarchical religions, such as Catholic, Muslim and Orthodox, delineate the strict, vertical bonds of authority that can help to instill the order and structure favored in a culture with a high UA score.

Following El Ghoul and Zheng (2016), Li, Griffin, Yue and Zhao (2013) and Kwok and Tadesse (2006), we employ two religion-based variables – a country's population percentage of hierarchical religions (*Hierarchical religion*) and its population percentage of other religions (*Protestantism*)[34] – as our UA instruments.[35]

[34] Protestantism is a major branch of Christianity that began in the 16th century during the Reformation, led by people like Martin Luther and John Calvin. Today, it includes many groups, such as Lutheran, Calvinist, Anglican, and Baptist churches.

[35] Nash and Patel (2019) showed that these two religion-based instrumental variables were strongly associated with UA, and thereby they appeared to satisfy the relevance condition required of good instruments.

6.2.3 IV Regression Results

The two-stage least squares (2SLS) estimation results are reported in Table 8. The left-hand panel presents the IV results for Long-Term Orientation (LTO), while the right-hand panel reports those for Uncertainty Avoidance (UA).

Table 8 Two-stage IV regressions

This table reports results for the two-stage IV regression for LTO and UA. In the first-stage regression, LTO (UA) is regressed on two instruments, genetic distance and linguistic distance (an instrument, hierarchical religions), and the included control variables. The F-statistic of instrument strength tests for joint significance of the instruments with null hypothesis that the instrument is weak. In the second-stage regression, the main independent variables are the predicted LTO (UA) obtained from the first-stage regression. The Hansen J-statistics, which are chi-squared distributed, is used to test overidentifying restrictions under the null hypothesis that the error term is uncorrelated with the instruments. Robust standard errors clustered at the country level are in parentheses. Significance at the 10%, 5%, and 1% level is indicated by *, **, ***, respectively.

			First-stage	**Second-stage**	**First-stage**	**Second-stage**
Variables	*LTO*	*LTO*	*LTO*	*Private saving rates*	*UA*	*Private saving rates*
$\widehat{LTO}$				0.244***		
				(0.066)		
Genetic Distance	-7.868***		-8.006***			
	(1.374)		(1.589)			
Linguistic Distance		-14.342**	-1.965			
		(7.058)	(6.947)			
$\widehat{UA}$						-0.258**
						(0.127)
Hierarchical Religions					0.340***	
					(0.116)	
Ln (Real Per Capita GPDI)	-0.030	-0.006	0.025	0.050***	-0.071	0.002
	(0.042)	(0.048)	(0.043)	(0.017)	(0.088)	(0.034)
Real Growth Rate of Per Capita GPDI	0.164**	0.208*	0.055	0.116***	0.318	0.511***
	(0.080)	(0.119)	(0.067)	(0.042)	(0.248)	(0.135)
Ln (Terms of Trade)	0.018	-0.040	0.017	0.015	-0.026	0.012
	(0.038)	(0.041)	(0.033)	(0.027)	(0.139)	(0.040)
Real Deposit Rate	0.165	-0.228	0.070	-0.177	0.508	-0.123
	(0.197)	(0.264)	(0.222)	(0.128)	(0.587)	(0.224)
Flow of Private Sector Credit/GPDI	0.019	0.037	0.001	-0.098***	-0.198**	-0.116***
	(0.076)	(0.066)	(0.059)	(0.031)	(0.090)	(0.045)
Inflation	-0.083	-0.666**	-0.170	-0.025	1.596***	0.306
	(0.243)	(0.311)	(0.256)	(0.144)	(0.547)	(0.350)

Old Age	2.129^{***}	1.522^{***}	2.122^{***}	-0.891^{***}	1.234	-0.007
Dependency Ratio	(0.341)	(0.531)	(0.348)	(0.184)	(1.032)	(0.284)
Share of Urban	0.122	-0.032	0.199	-0.098^{**}	0.262	-0.100
Population	(0.154)	(0.177)	(0.158)	(0.046)	(0.295)	(0.113)
Life Expectancy	-0.656	-0.058	-1.496^{***}	0.388^{*}	0.762	0.732
	(0.416)	(0.459)	(0.509)	(0.225)	(1.950)	(0.751)
Sovereign Debt	-3.637	-1.825	-2.584	0.823	-1.510	-0.138
Crisis	(3.566)	(5.018)	(3.657)	(2.285)	(5.480)	(2.420)
Intercept	98.545^{***}	65.781^{*}	105.825^{***}	-43.028^{**}	11.911	-13.234
	(31.149)	(36.099)	(34.810)	(17.657)	(80.672)	(39.106)
N	1763	1611	1536	1536	978	978
Year dummy	yes	yes	yes	yes	yes	yes
Adj. R^2	0.503	0.282	0.535	0.232	0.310	0.322
Hansen J statistic (p-value)				0.050(0.823)		
First-stage F statistic (p-value)				22.433(0.000)		8.572(0.006)

(1) Instrumental Variable Results for LTO

In the first-stage regression, the two instruments—Genetic Distance and Linguistic Distance—are both negatively correlated with LTO. The estimated coefficients are statistically significant at the 1% and 5% levels, respectively. These results are consistent with the expectation that countries genetically and linguistically closer to the LTO frontier country exhibit stronger long-term orientation.

To improve efficiency, we use both instruments jointly in the first-stage regression. The F-statistic for the joint significance of the instruments is 22.433 (p-value = 0.000), which comfortably exceeds conventional thresholds used to detect weak instruments. Therefore, the null hypothesis of weak instruments is clearly rejected, supporting the relevance condition.

In the second-stage regression, where LTO is instrumented using the predicted values from the first stage, the estimated coefficient on instrumented LTO remains positive and statistically significant. Both the sign and significance are consistent with the baseline OLS results, reinforcing the conclusion that higher LTO leads to higher private saving rates.

Because more than one instrument is used for LTO, we conduct an overidentification test to assess the validity of the exclusion restriction. The Hansen J-statistic equals 0.050, with a p-value of 0.823. Since we fail to reject the null hypothesis that the instruments are valid, the overidentifying restrictions are supported by the data. This result suggests that Genetic Distance and Linguistic Distance affect private saving rates only through their impact on LTO.

(2) Instrumental Variable Results for UA

The right-hand panel of Table 8 reports the IV results for Uncertainty Avoidance (UA). In this specification, Hierarchical Religion is used as the instrument for UA.

The first-stage regression shows that Hierarchical Religion is positively and statistically significantly correlated with UA at the 1% level.[36] The F-statistic for the instrument is 8.572 (p-value = 0.006), indicating that the instrument is statistically relevant. Although the F-statistic is lower than in the LTO specification, it exceeds conventional significance levels, and the null hypothesis of a weak instrument is rejected.

In the second-stage regression, the coefficient on the instrumented UA remains negative and statistically significant, consistent with the baseline OLS findings. This result confirms that higher uncertainty avoidance is associated with lower private saving rates and strengthens the causal interpretation of the earlier results.

Overall, the IV estimations corroborate the baseline regression findings. After accounting for potential endogeneity, the positive effect of LTO and the negative effect of UA on private saving rates remain robust. These results provide stronger evidence that deep-rooted cultural characteristics exert a causal influence on cross-country differences in private saving behavior.

---

[36] Of the two UA instruments, the two-stage IV results showed that the IV requirement was satisfied only by the *Hierarchical religion* instrument; thus, the results on *Protestantism* are not reported in Table 8.

7. CONCLUSIONS

Economists have long attempted to explain disparities in international saving behavior through differences in economic factors, including demographics, income levels, income growth, inflation, income inequality, and social security systems. While such explanations have provided partial insights, they have largely failed to account for persistent cross-country differences in private saving rates. This has led researchers to consider whether cultural factors, rather than purely economic ones, may drive saving behavior.

Despite growing recognition of culture's potential role, prior studies have faced significant challenges, including difficulties in measuring culture, addressing endogeneity, and accessing comprehensive datasets. The present study advances the literature by addressing these limitations in two main ways. First, we employ a substantially larger dataset covering 84 countries from 1981 to 2012, alongside Hofstede et al.'s (2010) six cultural dimensions, to examine the influence of culture on private saving rates. Our findings indicate that Long-Term Orientation (LTO) and Uncertainty Avoidance (UA) exert strong and statistically significant effects (at the 1% level) on private saving rates worldwide, while Indulgence versus Restraint (IVR) has a weaker, yet still significant, influence (at the 5% level). In addition, countries with Confucian norms consistently exhibit higher private saving rates.

The second aim of the study is to address the enduring puzzle of why China, Japan, and other East Asian countries save so consistently and at such high levels. Our results suggest that the combination of Confucian norms, high LTO, and low UA explains both the magnitude and persistence of high private saving rates in these countries. Specifically, Confucian values and a strong long-term orientation encourage higher savings, while low uncertainty avoidance ensures that savings behavior remains resilient, even during periods of economic uncertainty.

Beyond East Asia, our analysis shows that a restrained culture (low IVR) positively influences private saving rates worldwide, albeit to a more modest degree. For example, "other Asian countries," which are predominantly shaped by hierarchical religions (e.g., Islam, Judaism, Orthodoxy), display the lowest IVR scores and correspondingly rank second-highest in private saving rates, further supporting the role of cultural norms in shaping savings behavior. Furthermore, cultural indulgence (high IVR) combined with a short-term orientation (low LTO) helps explain why Africa has the lowest private saving rate, while South America ranks second lowest.

Finally, to address concerns of omitted variables, simultaneity, and measurement error in cultural proxies, we employ an instrumental variable (IV) approach using Genetic Distance and Linguistic Distance for LTO and Hierarchical Religion for UA. The IV results confirm that our main findings are robust to endogeneity concerns, providing strong causal evidence that culture is a key determinant of international differences in private saving behavior.

Overall, this study demonstrates that deep-rooted cultural factors—particularly Confucianism, long-term orientation, low uncertainty avoidance, and self-restraint—play a dominant role in shaping private saving rates globally. These findings contribute to a better understanding of cross-country saving disparities and offer valuable insights for policymakers seeking to influence household savings behavior through culturally informed strategies.

REFERENCES

Adams, F.G. and P.A. Prazmowski (2003), 'Why are Saving Rates in East Asia so High? Reviving the Life Cycle Hypothesis', *Empirical Economics*, **28**(2): 275-89.

Aggarwal, R., C. Kearney and B.M. Lucey (2012), 'Gravity and Culture in Foreign Portfolio Investment', *Journal of Banking and Finance*, **36**(2): 525-38.

Aghion, P., Y. Algan, P. Cahuc and A. Shleifer (2010), 'Regulation and Distrust', *Quarterly Journal of Economics*, **125**(3): 1015-49.

Ahern, K.R., D. Daminelli and C. Fracassi (2015), 'Lost in Translation? The Effect of Cultural Values on Mergers around the World', *Journal of Financial Economics*, **117**(1): 165-89.

Alipour, A. and Yaprak, A. (2024), 'National culture and firms' cash holdings: The role of indulgence and its boundaries', *Journal of Business Research*, 172: 114414.

Alipour, A. and Yaprak, A. (2022), 'Indulgence and risk-taking behavior of firms: Direct and interactive influences', *Journal of International Management*, 28: 100945.

Asterious, D. and S.G. Hall (2001), *Applied Econometrics*, 2nd edition, New York: Palgrave Macmillan.

Bande, R. and D. Riveiro (2013), 'Private Saving Rates and Macroeconomic Uncertainty: Evidence from Spanish Regional Data', *Economic and Social Review*, **44**(3): 323-49.

Bailliu, J.N. and H. Reisen (1998), 'Do Funded Pensions Contribute to Higher Aggregate Savings? A Cross-country Analysis', *Review of World Economics*, **134**(4): 692-711.

Barro, R.J. and R.M. McCleary (2003), 'Religion and Economic Growth across Countries', *American Sociological Review*, **68**(5): 760-81.

Beugelsdijk, S., R. Maseland and A. Van Hoorn (2015), 'Are Scores on Hofstede's Dimensions of National Culture Stable over time? A Cohort Analysis', *Global Strategy Journal*, **5**: 223-240.

Blanchard, O.J. and F. Giavazzi (2006), 'Rebalancing Growth in China: A Three-handed Approach', *China and World Economy*, **14**(4): 1-20.

Bonham, C. and C. Wiemer (2013), 'Chinese Saving Dynamics: The Impact of GDP Growth and the Dependent Share', *Oxford Economic Papers,* **65**: 173-96.

Boubakri, N., A. Mirzaei and A. Samet (2017), 'National Culture and Bank Performance: Evidence from the Recent Financial Crisis', *Journal of Financial Stability*, **29**: 36-56.

Bosworth, B.P. (1993), '*Saving and Investment in a Global Economy*, Washington, DC: Brookings Institution.

Bova, F. and M.D. Vance (2019), 'Uncertainty Avoidance and the Timing of Employee Stock Option Exercise', *Journal of International Business Studies*, **50**(5): 740-57.

Bryan, S., R. Nash and A. Patel (2015), 'The Effect of Cultural Distance on Contracting Decisions: The Case of Executive Compensation', *Journal of Corporate Finance*, **33**: 180-95.

Carroll, C.D., B.K. Rhee and C. Rhee (1994), 'Are there Cultural Effects on Saving? Some Cross-sectional Evidence', *Quarterly Journal of Economics*, **109**(3): 685-99.

Carroll, C.D., B.K. Rhee and C. Rhee (1999), 'Does Cultural Origin Affect Saving Behavior? Evidence from Immigrants', *Economic Development and Cultural Change*, **48**(1): 33-50.

Cavalli-Sforza, L. (2001), '*Genes, Peoples and Languages*, Berkeley, CA: University of California Press.

Cavalli-Sforza, L., P. Menozzi and P. Piazza (1994), *The History and Geography of Human Genes*, Princeton, NJ: Princeton University Press.

Chao, C., J. Laffargue and E.S. Yu (2011), 'The Chinese Saving Puzzle and the Life-cycle Hypothesis: A Revaluation', *China Economic Review*, **22**(1): 108-20.

Chamon, M. D. and E. S. Prasad (2010), 'Why Are Saving Rates of Urban Households in China Rising?' *American Economic Journal: Macroeconomics*, **2** (1): 93–130.

Chamon, M., K. Liu and E.S. Prasad (2013), 'Income Uncertainty and Household

Savings in China', *Journal of Development Economics*, **105**(289): 164-77.

Chang, C. and S. Lin (2015), 'The Effects of National Culture and Behavioral Pitfalls on Investors' Decision-making: Herding Behavior in International Stock Markets', *International Review of Economics and Finance*, **37**: 380-92.

Chang, K. and A. Noorbakhsh (2009), 'Does National Culture Affect International Corporate Cash Holdings', *Journal of Multinational Financial Management*, **19**(5): 323-42.

Chen, K., A. Imrohoroglu and S. Imrohoroglu (2006), 'The Japanese Saving Rate', *American Economic Review*, **96**(5): 1850-58.

Chen, L., Z. Jin, Y. Ma and H. Xu (2019), 'Confucianism, Openness to the West and Corporate Investment Efficiency', *European Financial Management*, **25**(3): 554-90.

Chen, Y., P.Y. Dou, S.G. Rhee, C. Truong and M. Veeraraghavan (2015), 'National Culture and Corporate Cash Holdings around the World', *Journal of Banking and Finance*, **50**(Jan.): 1-18.

Chu, T. and Q. Wen (2017), 'Can Income Inequality Explain China's Saving Puzzle?', *International Review of Economics and Finance*, **52**: 222-35.

Chui, A.C. and C.C. Kwok (2008), 'National Culture and Life Insurance Consumption', *Journal of International Business Studies*, **39**(1): 88-101.

Cigno, A. and F.C. Rosati (1997), 'Rise and Fall of the Japanese Saving Rate: The Role of Social Security and Intra-family Transfers', *Japan and the World Economy*, **9**(1): 81-92.

Costa, B.A., A.J. Crawford and K. Jakob (2013), 'Does Culture Influence IPO Underpricing', *Journal of Multinational Financial Management*, **23**(1): 113-23.

Dayal-Gulati, A. and C. Thimann (1997), *Saving in Southeast Asia and Latin America Compared: Searching for Policy Lessons*, IMF Working Paper No. 97/110.

Dang, H.D. and G. Partington (2020), 'Sovereign Ratings and National Culture', *Pacific-basin Finance Journal*, **60**: Article 101296.

Dow, D. and A.R. Karunaratna (2006), 'Developing a Multidimensional Instrument to Measure Psychic Distance Stimuli', *Journal of International Business Studies*, **37**(5): 578-602.

Du, X. (2015), 'Does Confucianism Reduce Minority Shareholder Expropriation? Evidence from China', *Journal of Business Ethics*, **132**(4): 661-716.

Du, X. (2016), 'Does Confucianism Reduce Board Gender Diversity? Firm-level Evidence from China', *Journal of Business Ethics*, **136**(2): 399-436.

Edwards, S. (1996), 'Why are Latin America's Savings Rates so Low? An International Comparative Analysis', *Journal of Development Economics*, **51**(1): 5-44.

El Ghoul, S. and X. Zheng (2016), 'Trade Credit Provision and National Culture', *Journal of Corporate Finance*, **41**, 475-501.

Eun, C.S., L. Wang and S.C. Xiao (2015), 'Culture and R2', *Journal of Financial Economics*, **115**(2): 283-303.

Ferris, S.P., N. Jayaraman and S. Sabherwal (2013), 'CEO Overconfidence and International Merger and Acquisition Activity', *Journal of Financial and Quantitative Analysis*, **48**(1): 137-64.

Franke, R.H., G. Hofstede and M.H. Bond (1991), 'Cultural Roots of Economic Performance: A Research Note', *Strategic Management Journal*, **12**(S1): 165-73.

Gorodnichenko, Y. and G. Roland (2017), 'Culture, Institutions and the Wealth of Nations', *Review of Economics and Statistics*, **99**(3): 402-16.

Grigoli, F., A. Herman and K. Schmidt-Hebbel (2018), 'Saving in the World', *World Development*, **104**: 257-70.

Gu, X., P.S. Tam, G. Li and Q. Zhao (2020), 'An Alternative Explanation for High Saving in China: Rising Inequality', *International Review of Economics and Finance*, **69**:1082-1094

Guo, N. and Tu, A.H. (2023), 'Does Culture Explain the High Private Saving Behavior in East Asian Countries? Further Evidence', *The Singapore Economic Review*, **68**(2): 413-456.

Guiso, L., P. Sapienza and L. Zingales (2016), 'Long-Term persistence', *Journal of the European Economic Association*, **14**(6): 1401-36.

Gutiérrez, M.A. (2007), 'Savings in Latin America after the Mid-1990s: Determinants, Constraints and Policies', *CEPAL Serie Macroeconomía del*

Desarrollo, Vol. 57.

Hao, J., Z. Wang, X. Zhang, F. He and X. Chen (2024), 'Culture Imprint and Gambling Preference: Evidence from Individual Investors' Trading in the Chinese Stock Market', *Emerging Markets Review*, **60**: 101136.

Haq, M., D. Hu, R.W. Faff and S. Pathan (2017), 'New Evidence on National Culture and Bank Capital Structure', *Pacific-basin Finance Journal*, **50**: 41-64.

Hayashi, F. (1986), 'Why is Japan's Saving Rate So Apparently High?', *NBER Macroeconomics Annual*, **1**: 147-234.

He, X. and Y. Cao (2007), 'Understanding High Saving Rates in China', *China and World Economy*, **15**(1): 1-13.

Hofstede, G. (1980), *Culture's Consequences: International Differences in Work-related Values*, Beverly Hills, CA: Sage Publications.

Hofstede, G. (1983), 'National Cultures Revisited', *Cross-cultural Research*, **18**(4): 285-305.

Hofstede, G. (1991), *Culture and Organizations: Software of the Mind*, New York: McGraw Hill.

Hofstede, G. (2001), *Culture's Consequences: Comparing Values, Behavior, Institutions and Organizations across Nations*, Beverly Hills, CA: Sage Publications.

Hofstede, G. and G.J. Hofstede (2005), *Culture and Organizations: Software of the Mind, Intercultural Cooperation and Its Importance for Survival*, 2nd Edition., New York: McGraw Hill.

Hofstede, G. and M.H. Bond (1988), 'The Confucius Connection: From Cultural Roots to Economic Growth', *Organizational Dynamics*, **16**(4): 5-21.

Hofstede, G., G.J. Hofstede and M. Minkov (2010), *Culture and Organizations: Software of the Mind, Intercultural Cooperation and Its Importance for Survival*, 3rd Edition., New York: McGraw Hill.

Horioka, C. Y. (2019), 'Are the Japanese Unique? Evidence from Saving and Bequest Behavior', *The Singapore Economic Review*, **64**(1): 5-22.

Horioka, C. Y. (2021), 'Is the Selfish Life-Cycle Model More Applicable in Japan and, if So, Why? A Literature Survey', *Review of Economics of the Household*,

19(1): 157-187.

Horioka, C.Y. (1990), 'Why is Japan's Household Saving Rate So High? A Literature Survey', *Journal of the Japanese and International Economies*, **4**(1): 49-92.

Horioka, C.Y. and J. Wan (2007), 'The Determinants of Household Saving in China: A Dynamic Panel Analysis of Provincial Data', *Journal of Money, Credit and Banking*, **39**(8): 2077-96.

Horioka, C.Y. and A. Terada-Hagiwara (2012), 'The Determinants and Long-term Projections of Saving Rates in Developing Asia', *Japan and the World Economy*, **24**(2): 128-37.

Huang, Y., L. Jin and Y. Qian (2013), 'Does Ethnicity Pay? Evidence from Overseas Chinese FDI in China', *Review of Economics and Statistics*, **95**(3): 868-83.

Kanagaretnam, K., C.Y. Him and G.J. Hobo (2014), 'Influence of National Culture on Accounting Conservatism and Risk-taking in the Banking Industry', *Accounting Review*, **89**(3): 1115-49.

Kaufmann, D., A. Kraay and M. Mastruzzi (2003), 'Governance Matters III: Governance Indicators for 1996-2002', *World Bank Working Paper #3106*.

Kraay, A. (2000), 'Household Saving in China', *World Bank Economic Review*, **14**(3): 545-70.

Kung, K.S. and C. Ma (2014), 'Can Cultural Norms Reduce Conflicts? Confucianism and Peasant Rebellions in Qing China', *Journal of Development Economics*, **111**: 132-49.

Kwok, C.C. and S.A. Tadesse (2006), 'National Culture and Financial Systems', *Journal of International Business Studies*, **37**(2): 227-47.

La Porta, R., F. Lopez-de-Silane, A. Shleifer and R.W. Vishny (1997), 'Trust in Large Organizations', *American Economic Review*, **87**(2): 333-8.

Leland, H.E. (1968), 'Saving and Uncertainty: The Precautionary Demand for Saving', *Quarterly Journal of Economics*, **82**(3): 465-73.

Levenko, N. (2020), 'Perceived Uncertainty as a Key Driver of Household Saving', *International Review of Economics and Finance*, **65**: 126-45.

Li, H. and H.F. Zou (2004), 'Savings and Income Distribution', *Annals of Economics and Finance*, **5**(2): 245-70.

Li, K., D. Griffin, H. Yue and L. Zhao (2013), 'How Does Culture Influence Corporate Risk-taking?', *Journal of Corporate Finance*, **23**(23): 1-22.

Li, Y. and S.A. Zahra (2012), 'Formal Institutions, Culture and Venture Capital Activity: A Cross-country Analysis', *Journal of Business Venturing*, **27**(1): 95-111.

Lievenbruck, M. and T.E. Schmid (2014), 'Why Do Firms (Not) Hedge? - Novel Evidence on Cultural Influence', *Journal of Corporate Finance*, **25**: 92-106.

Loayza, N.V., K. Schmidt-Hebbel and L. Servén (2000), 'What Drives Private Saving Across the World?', *Review of Economics and Statistics*, **82**(2):165-81.

Lopez, H., K. Schmidthebbel and L. Servén (2000), 'How Effective is Fiscal Policy in Raising National Saving', *Review of Economics and Statistics*, **82**(2): 226-38.

Meng, X. (2003), 'Unemployment, Consumption Smoothing and Precautionary Saving in Urban China', *Journal of Comparative Economics*, **31**(3): 465-85.

Modigliani, F. and S.L. Cao (2004), 'The Chinese Saving Puzzle and the Life-cycle Hypothesis', *Journal of Economic Literature*, **42**(1): 145-70.

Mody, A., F. Ohnsorge and D. Sandri (2012), 'Precautionary Savings in the Great Recession', *IMF Economic Review*, **60**(1): 114-38.

Nash, R.C. and A. Patel (2019), 'Instrumental Variable Analysis and the Role of National Culture in Corporate Finance', *Financial Management*, **48**(2): 385-416.

Orlova, S., R.P. Rao and T. Kang (2017), 'National Culture and the Valuation of Cash Holdings', *Journal of Business Finance and Accounting*, **44**: 236-70.

Poston, D.L. and J.H. Wong (2016), 'The Chinese Diaspora: The Current Distribution of the Overseas Chinese Population', *Chinese Journal of Sociology*, **2**(3): 348-73.

Rauch, J.E. and V. Trindade (2002), 'Ethnic Chinese Networks in International Trade', *Review of Economics and Statistics*, **84**(1): 116-30.

Rieger, M.O., M. Wang and T. Hens (2015), 'Risk Preferences Around the World', *Management Science*, **61**(3): 637-48.

Schmidt-Hebbel, K. and L. Servén (2000), 'Does Income Inequality Raise Aggregate Saving', *Journal of Development Economics*, **61**(2): 417-46.

Siegel, J.I., A.N. Licht and S.H. Schwartz (2013), 'Egalitarianism, Cultural Distance and Foreign Direct Investment: A New Approach', *Organization Science*, **24**(4): 1174-94.

Spolaore, E. and R. Wacziarg (2009), 'The Diffusion of Development', *Quarterly Journal of Economics*, **124**(2): 469-529.

Spolaore, E. and R. Wacziarg (2018), 'Ancestry and Development: New Evidence', *Journal of Applied Econometrics*, **33**: 748-62.

Tan, G., C.S. Cheong and R. Zurbruegg (2019), 'National Culture and Individual Trading Behavior', *Journal of Banking and Finance*, **106**(9): 357-70.

Tang, L. and P. Koveos (2008), 'A Framework to Update Hofstede's Cultural Value Indices: Economic Dynamics and Institutional Stability', *Journal of International Business Studies*, 39(6): 1045-1063.

Wang, D. and O.A. Esqueda (2014), 'National Cultural Effects on Leverage Decisions: Evidence from Emerging-market ADRs', *Research in International Business and Finance*, **31**(May): 152-77.

Wei, S. and X. Zhang (2011), 'The Competitive Saving Motive: Evidence from Rising Sex Ratios and Savings Rates in China', *Journal of Political Economy*, **119**(3): 511-64.

Williamson, O.E. (2000), 'The New Institutional Economics: Taking Stock, Looking Ahead', *Journal of Economic Literature*, **38**(3): 595-613.

Ye, D., S. Pan, Y. Lian and Y.- K. Ng (2020), 'Culture and Savings: Why do Asians Save More?', *The Singapore Economic Review*, Online, 1-31.

Yeh, R. and J.J. Lawrence (1995), 'Individualism and Confucian Dynamism: A Note on Hofstede's Cultural Root to Economic Growth', *Journal of International Business Studies*, **26**(3): 655-69.

Zheng, X., S.E. Ghoul, O. Guedhami and C.C.Y. Kwok (2012), 'National Culture and Corporate Debt Maturity', *Journal of Banking and Finance*, **36**(2): 468-88.

APPENDIX

Table A1 The result of baseline regression (Equation (1)) using five cultural dimensions in Hofstede and Hofstede (2005) for the first sub-sample period (1981-2000)

This table reports the result of baseline regression as the following equation

$$Private\_Saving\_Rate_{it} = \alpha + \beta CulturalProxy_i + \gamma Control_{it} + \varphi_t + \varepsilon_{it}$$

The scores of five cultural dimensions in Hofstede and Hofstede (2005) are used as cultural proxies. The dependent variable is private saving rates. All parameters are estimated by using pooled ordinary least squares (OLS) with standard errors adjusted for clustering by country. Cultural proxies include scores of LTO on 32 countries and scores of UA, MAS, IND and PD on 54 countries. Robust standard errors clustered at the country level are in parentheses. Significance at the 10%, 5%, and 1% level is indicated by *, **, ***, respectively.

Variables	**(1)**	**(2)**	**(3)**	**(4)**	**(5)**	**(6)**
LTO	0.176***					0.172***
	(0.053)					(0.051)
UA		-0.065*				-0.036
		(0.038)				(0.042)
MAS			-0.016			
			(0.034)			
IND				-0.019		
				(0.041)		
PD					0.071**	
					(0.032)	
Ln (Real Per Capita GPDI)	0.053**	0.053***	0.049**	0.047**	0.049**	0.058**
	(0.020)	(0.019)	(0.022)	(0.021)	(0.020)	(0.022)
Real Growth Rate of Per Capita GPDI	0.212**	0.368***	0.371***	0.369***	0.371***	0.310***
	(0.077)	(0.064)	(0.069)	(0.067)	(0.069)	(0.066)
Ln (Terms of Trade)	0.104**	0.010	0.010	0.009	0.006	0.127**
	(0.040)	(0.051)	(0.050)	(0.053)	(0.054)	(0.050)
Real Deposit Rate	-0.157	-0.247*	-0.314**	-0.317**	-0.329**	-0.186
	(0.160)	(0.134)	(0.141)	(0.144)	(0.140)	(0.164)
Flow of Private Sector Credit/GPDI	-0.051	-0.014	0.013	0.014	0.022	-0.061
	(0.046)	(0.057)	(0.066)	(0.066)	(0.067)	(0.043)
Inflation	-0.079	-0.203	-0.333***	-0.348***	-0.365***	0.009
	(0.142)	(0.123)	(0.113)	(0.119)	(0.106)	(0.156)
Old Age Dependency Ratio	-0.154	-0.222	-0.256	-0.202	-0.132	-0.137
	(0.306)	(0.206)	(0.231)	(0.206)	(0.217)	(0.285)
Share of Urban Population	-0.062	-0.099*	-0.078	-0.071	-0.062	-0.083
	(0.071)	(0.052)	(0.052)	(0.054)	(0.049)	(0.080)
Intercept	-67.874***	-10.458	-8.941	-8.248	-14.850	-80.995***
	(14.204)	(26.367)	(26.753)	(27.287)	(28.619)	(22.427)
N	483	712	712	712	712	467

Year dummy	yes	yes	yes	yes	yes	yes
Adj. R^2	0.510	0.319	0.283	0.283	0.307	0.488

Table A2 The result of baseline regression (Equation (1)) using six cultural dimensions in Hofstede et al. (2010) for the second sub-sample period (2001-2012)

This table reports the result of baseline regression as the following equation

$$Private\_Saving\_Rate_{it} = \alpha + \beta CulturalProxy_i + \gamma Control_{it} + \varphi_t + \varepsilon_{it}$$

The scores of six cultural dimensions in Hofstede et al. (2010) are used as cultural proxies. The dependent variable is private saving rates. All parameters are estimated by using pooled ordinary least squares (OLS) with standard errors adjusted for clustering by country. Cultural proxies include scores of *LTO* on 84 countries, scores of *UA*, *MAS*, *IND* and *PD* on 61 countries and scores of IVR on 81 countries. Robust standard errors clustered at the country level are in parentheses. Significance at the 10%, 5%, and 1% level is indicated by *, **, ***, respectively.

Variables	(1)	(2)	(3)	(4)	(5)	(6)	(7)
LTO	0.109**						0.095**
	(0.048)						(0.045)
UA		-0.163***					-0.148***
		(0.037)					(0.031)
MAS			-0.009				
			(0.045)				
IND				0.030			
				(0.051)			
PD					-0.000		
					(0.046)		
IVR						-0.076	
						(0.047)	
Ln (Real Per Capita GPDI)	0.069***	0.035*	0.059***	0.055***	0.059***	0.075***	0.040**
	(0.015)	(0.020)	(0.021)	(0.021)	(0.020)	(0.017)	(0.018)
Real Growth Rate of Per Capita GPDI	0.180**	0.270**	0.332**	0.339**	0.335**	0.201**	0.209**
	(0.078)	(0.126)	(0.160)	(0.151)	(0.148)	(0.096)	(0.102)
Ln (Terms of Trade)	0.090**	0.008	-0.011	-0.010	-0.010	0.084**	0.027
	(0.036)	(0.035)	(0.042)	(0.042)	(0.042)	(0.038)	(0.032)
Real Deposit Rate	-0.347**	0.020	-0.103	-0.114	-0.102	-0.345**	0.045
	(0.152)	(0.161)	(0.201)	(0.200)	(0.200)	(0.152)	(0.167)
Flow of Private Sector Credit/GPDI	-0.073*	-0.088*	-0.039	-0.038	-0.036	-0.067	-0.094**
	(0.039)	(0.044)	(0.067)	(0.059)	(0.060)	(0.043)	(0.041)
Inflation	-0.193	0.027	-0.169	-0.164	-0.170	-0.220	0.043
	(0.221)	(0.228)	(0.264)	(0.260)	(0.265)	(0.216)	(0.242)
Old Age Dependency Ratio	-0.747***	-0.172	-0.471**	-0.495**	-0.465**	-0.656***	-0.338**
	(0.167)	(0.152)	(0.187)	(0.188)	(0.185)	(0.170)	(0.140)
Share of Urban Population	-0.058	-0.067	-0.116**	-0.114**	-0.115**	-0.046	-0.067
	(0.052)	(0.050)	(0.054)	(0.053)	(0.054)	(0.058)	(0.050)
Intercept	-66.714***	7.517	-7.204	-5.636	-7.531	-62.766***	-8.224
	(17.343)	(22.772)	(25.571)	(24.676)	(25.736)	(18.288)	(20.739)

N	964	706	706	706	706	929	706
Year dummy	yes	yes	yes	yes	yes	yes	yes
Adj. R^2	0.256	0.294	0.127	0.130	0.126	0.239	0.341

Declaration of AI-assisted technologies in the writing process:

During the preparation of this work, the authors used ChatGPT to proofread the manuscript and enhance its readability and clarity. The authors assume full responsibility for the content of the publication.